D1824481

An Outlaw is a person who refuses to be governed by the established rules, practices or traditions.

An Outlaw changes the way the game is played, forever.

OUTLAW

WALDO

OUTLAW

FIGHT FOR YOUR CUSTOMERS & SELL WITHOUT FEAR

TRENT LEYSHAN

WILEY

John Wiley & Sons, Australia, Ltd

First published in 2013 by
John Wiley & Sons Australia, Ltd
42 McDougall St, Milton Qld 4064

Office also in Melbourne

Typeset in 11.5/13 pt Bembo Std

© Wisdom Pearl Publishing Pty Ltd 2013

The moral rights of the author have been asserted

National Library of Australia Cataloguing-in-Publication data:

Author:	Leyshan, Trent.
Title:	Outlaw : fight for your customers and sell without fear/Trent Leyshan.
ISBN:	9781118524060 (pbk.)
Notes:	Includes index.
Subjects:	Selling.
	Sales personnel — Attitudes.
	Success in business.
Dewey Number:	658.85

All rights reserved. Except as permitted under the *Australian Copyright Act 1968* (for example, a fair dealing for the purposes of study, research, criticism or review), no part of this book may be reproduced, stored in a retrieval system, communicated or transmitted in any form or by any means without prior written permission. All inquiries should be made to the publisher at the address above.

Cover design by Paul McCarthy

Cover image by © iStockphoto/Sankai

Author photograph © Timothy Herbert

Printed in China by Printplus Limited

10 9 8 7 6 5 4 3 2 1

Disclaimer
The material in this publication is of the nature of general comment only, and does not represent professional advice. It is not intended to provide specific guidance for particular circumstances and it should not be relied on as the basis for any decision to take action or not take action on any matter which it covers. Readers should obtain professional advice where appropriate, before making any such decision. To the maximum extent permitted by law, the author and publisher disclaim all responsibility and liability to any person, arising directly or indirectly from any person taking or not taking action based on the information in this publication.

This book is dedicated to my little Outlaws,
Tristan, Skye and Trinity

Contents

About the author

Trent Leyshan is the founder and CEO of international sales training and development company *BOOM!* As the lead consultant and facilitator, he partners with some of the world's most dynamic sales and service-driven companies. Clients include the National Australia Bank, Symbion Health, American Banknote, CSR and Crown Casino, to name a few.

Trent combines his unique experiences in business, rigorous research and new insights with fresh, interactive delivery methods that inspire action and lasting change in behaviour. He works with hundreds of salespeople across a broad range of industries every year. He designs and delivers sales seminars and in-house training programs across Australia, New Zealand and Asia.

Early in his career, Trent was the head spruiker and national sales manager at Big Kev's. Under the guidance of mentor Kevin McQuay (Big Kev), Australia's most flamboyant TV sales personality, he learned and developed his sales and presentation skills.

He has since led sales teams in award-winning advertising and online marketing agencies. He has transformed two companies from lounge-room operations into industry leaders. He is the author of *The Naked Salesman* (www.thenakedsalesman.com), and a sought-after speaker and contributor to various media on sales strategy and sales leadership.

For more information visit www.boomsales.com.au

Or connect with Trent here:
Facebook: www.facebook.com/trentleyshan
Twitter: @trentleyshan
LinkedIn: www.linkedin.com/in/trentleyshan

Introduction

The winds of change are howling more violently than ever. World money-making markets resemble the Wild West, with ethics being cast aside in the name of self-preservation and personal gain. The dotcom bubble at the turn of last century, and more recently the global financial crises and European debt crisis, provide a damning case in point. Our commercial world is now interconnected, forever changing, making it more volatile and unpredictable. Today, sales professionals are faced with novel and obscure demands on their skills, resources and time. Marketing is now considered a jargon term used by old-schoolers, as social media sweeps us all off our feet. Genuine customer loyalty appears to be a token gesture from a distant past, as amplified competition across industries ensures the customer's bottom line is now constantly top-of-mind.

The internet has spectacularly changed the way we all conduct business. Customers can now find whatever they need with speed and precision. So much information and choice is readily available, and it's only a click away. As our business world spins faster and faster, we are all showered with the debris of outdated beliefs and redundant modes of operating. Most of us are left dizzy and out of breath. For others, the incessant battle with rejection leaves them downright nauseated. The business landscape is now a cold and confusing place, with the dazed players not knowing how to act, which way to go, or what approach to trust.

Who can predict what will happen three months from now, let alone in three years? 'Slash costs and discount!' is bellowed from the lofty heights of senior management, or 'How about we try this social media stuff?' Both approaches will end in frustration (enter the eerie strings of a sad violin), especially when you apply them from a place of desperation instead of inspiration. In these challenging times you need to do more of what works, not less. Innovate? Hell yes! Just remember the worst time to try something untested is when you most need to try something new, as the stakes are higher, the pressures intensified and the risks greater. It's time to get urgent now, before you really need to.

The sheriff is dead

The skills, strategies and behaviours required to succeed in sales many decades ago are noticeably different from those needed today. For the most part, customers were ill-informed, if not utterly ignorant, about the conniving ways of manipulative salespeople who directed their attention towards the unsophisticated. Sleazy cold-calling, ruthless closing techniques and slithering snake-oil salesmen thrived in this era. Towards the seventies and into the eighties competition had intensified and markets had begun to expand exponentially as mass media took hold. Sales professionals needed to evolve and invent new tactics to win customers. They soon realised that to be successful they had to embellish their relationships. Customers loved this treatment, and so they were easily seduced. Long lunches, promotions, discounts and free holidays were met with delight. Added to this, customers got a new sense of how they wanted to be treated, even though they were ultimately paying for it.

Just before the turn of this century — *kaboom!* The technology revolution and information age exploded into our lives. The internet propelled a distinct shift in consumer behaviour. Customers began to emerge from the dark ages. Buyers began to educate themselves, as a myriad of web and e-commerce sites sprouted up, and over time steadily began to change the way we all consume and buy things. Customers could now research and compare offers, and in many ways take back control of the buying process. They were also no longer willing to suffer fools or be treated like fools. The internet empowered and informed: the customer struck back and was no longer solely influenced by the salesperson.

We chart forward to today as the tempo of changes continues to accelerate. Business is even more complicated than it was a decade ago. True differentiation (to really stand out) is becoming increasingly challenging, if not impossible to assert. Markets such as property and real estate are stagnating on a global scale. The financial services space is morphing drastically while, sadly, industries like traditional retail that were too slow to adapt are now disintegrating.

A new force of influence is born

Despite these trying times and shifts in buyer behaviour, a specific type of sales professional is thriving. We are seeing a new force of influence emerge. These people are noticeably different from other sales professionals. They don't just sell a product or service: what they stand for, communicate and demonstrate transcends buying and selling, and influences their customers as if they were fighting for a worthy cause. They defy the rules and adopt a distinctive selling approach and apply it to forge ahead of their contemporaries. These extraordinarily influential sales leaders are called Outlaws.

Deeply passionate, and at times evangelistic, Outlaws know how to inspire and develop customer relationships, but they also recognise that's not nearly enough in the modern economy. Outlaws work by a set of insight-driven operating principles, seven to be exact, all neatly set out in this book.

These principles enable sales professionals to promote *outwardly* instead of being self-directed. The benefits of this approach are measured by customers no longer seeing the Outlaw as a salesperson: the Outlaw becomes instead a trusted ally—a person of influence they call on for critical advice to *lead* them through challenges and uncertainty. Think of some of the most trusted advisers you currently surround yourself with, such as doctors, mentors or accountants. None of these advisers need to sell you anything—instead, they inform and empower you with critical information that enhances your situation or wellbeing.

Outlaws put their customers first. They resist the urge to be the centre of attention. When you meet an Outlaw, it becomes clear that the engagement is all about you, not them. They will probe and ask meaningful questions that drill deep into your challenges and connect with your higher goals, desires and aspirations. They don't labour to be all things to all people: they are focused on and deeply committed to their field of endeavour, and willing to burrow underground to regroup, find and develop fresh impactful strategies. They are comfortable dwelling among real people, the crowd, to get a clear sense of what their customers really need. They are always listening, forever seeking an advantage to help their customers. Never content with what is, they search for what can and ultimately should be.

Outlaws don't possess endless budgets; they are forced to innovate, invent and try new things; and they don't just harness change—they drive it! Sure they take risks, and of course they get it wrong sometimes, but that never deters them from achieving their goals. They are not shy of calling in favours either, putting their ego aside to be vulnerable. They understand the power in collaborating with like-minded people, explicitly other Outlaws who are just as prepared to fight for their customers and deliver more! More choice, more service and more value are just some of the menu changes inspired by Outlaws.

As brazen and disruptive as Outlaws can be at times, they are equally conscious of how they impact others. They honour the little things, the simple stuff that is easy to do—yet easier to forget. Things that aren't at all strenuous to attain: all it takes is a genuine effort to make other people feel important and included. Oddly enough, it's these relatively easy things in life and business that are most challenging to master, like a smile for a stranger, a 'leave it to me' when something goes wrong, or a thoughtful ear when the time is right. Of course, we know all this stuff, but there's a proverbial grand canyon between knowing and demonstrating. This book aims to bridge this chasm.

Why you should keep reading

This book sets out in clear terms, in seven chapters, practical advice, tested strategies and activities to help harness the most critical skills, tools and behaviours to help you become a *real* person of influence in a manic-paced, ever-morphing commercial world. Whether you're a dogged sales veteran, a manager leading a team, an entrepreneur, a corporate high-flyer or simply a person who wants to be heard and taken seriously, this book speaks to the salesperson in you—a person that seeks to influence and make a difference. The insights and tools contained in this book, if applied correctly, will dramatically improve your individual and team performance. They are drawn from personal experiences and a career in selling at the coalface in some of the world's most dynamic and demanding industries. They come from collaborating with thousands of high-performing sales professionals over my career and hundreds of salespeople every year. They come from interviewing industry leaders and game changers. All these strategies are tested. All these methods are practical. Ready for you to learn, aim and fire! Make no mistake: when you finish reading this book you will be armed and dangerous—Most Wanted by your competitors and your peers, and, most importantly, by your customers.

To truly influence your customers you will need to know them more intimately, more deeply, than your competitors do. This type of personal engagement can only come about by genuinely caring about your customer and their best interests. It will mean defying rules to set fresh standards of excellence that guide your customers into new markets and possibilities. The Outlaw spirit is especially inspired when you transform key business functions and accelerate growth to create additional revenue streams and profit pathways. Outlaws understand that being chased by 'the popular opinion' and flying in the face of industry standards comes with the territory and is indeed part of the thrill.

Businesspeople often take their customer relationships for granted—to be precise, they don't always make the effort to evolve their customer relationships and move forward. Yet in a world that is now spinning faster than ever, they absolutely must. The relationship was once a sacred cow—now it's a given. Customers want *more* than just a shoulder to cry on; they also crave a trusted ally to help them successfully navigate the murky fog and burst through! This book contains powerful insights and case studies of the habits of some of today's most daring and successful businesspeople. These people are different, in fact, wonderfully so. It's their story and willingness to fight for what they truly believe in that makes them so influential and such inspiring role models.

CHAPTER 1

DARE TO PREPARE

Chance favours the prepared mind.

Louis Pasteur, 18th century French scientist

This timeless maxim is just as relevant today, perhaps even more so, given our busy lifestyles. When you are stressed, under constant pressure to meet deadlines and running late to meetings, chances are you're failing to prepare effectively, and in this state, your results will always correlate with your lack of preparation.

If it's not worth preparing for, why do it at all?

The old saying, perfect preparation is paramount for perfect performance, is accurate. How you prepare for each project or pitch will largely determine the goals you and your team set out to achieve. Let's be frank, admitting that your business is really not too dissimilar to most of your competitors is confronting. One, often overlooked, area in which you can differentiate yourself and move ahead of the other players, is how much time and thought you invest into what you do. Through well thought-out and habitual preparation, you can edge ahead of the pack by showing your customers just how much you care about creating the right outcomes for them. You also demonstrate that you take your time and theirs seriously.

The ancient Greek saying 'know thyself' has had a variety of meanings attributed to it in literature. The Suda, a 10th century AD dictionary of the ancient Greek lexicon, says: 'the proverb is applied to those whose boasts exceed what they are, and that "know thyself" is a warning to pay no attention to the opinion of the multitude'. Knowing your strengths and limitations is a key step in your preparation process. How you prepare yourself for each new business pitch, particularly when you are up against a worthy foe, will come down to how successfully you position your strengths in the mind of your client, and in a way that counteracts and overcomes your competitors.

Outlaws prepare diligently because they have to—they know just how strenuous it is to carry a sack loaded full with rejection over mountainous terrain every day. In many cases less is more, but when it comes to preparation more is more. Businesspeople often prepare ineffectively because they are time poor. In doing so they are erroneously judging their preparation time to be a luxury, preferring instead to hope for the best and wing it. A lack of preparation will breed incompetence. Similarly, a lack of preparation diminishes your credibility with peers and customers, and reduces your ability to execute at the highest level.

If you're stuck in a creative rut because you have been in the same role for too long, the best way forward is to keep pushing the boundaries for ways to improve, challenge and change things. This is where preparation comes in. You need to rethink what you're doing and come up with ways of seeing things from a fresh perspective and reframing old views into new and compelling strategies for your customers.

You can only achieve this by taking time out habitually and working on how your business or the entire industry can change and adapt or improve.

Save yourself first

Every time I take a domestic or international flight I am mildly entertained by the pre-flight safely spiel, which contains a statement that I believe transcends the aviation industry: 'In the event of an emergency, first place the oxygen mask over your own face, and only then over your child's.' To do so may initially appear as a selfish act, but it expresses the need to save yourself first in order to stay conscious and alert to save your most cherished. There is no shortage of people out there striving to save the world, and that's an admirable ambition—just make sure you put food on your own table first. You will need your strength if you are going to truly fight for your customers and create a business you are proud of. Over the years, I have met plenty of business professionals who are competent in their craft, yet they fail to demonstrate their own unique skills for their own commercial purposes. Think of a landscape gardener with a house surrounded with feral foliage, a dentist with pungent breath, or a search engine marketer who is not first page on Google. If these people fail to demonstrate their skills for themselves, what does that say about their commitment to their customers?

Where preparation meets opportunity

You are more influential and vastly more potent when you can successfully demonstrate how you personally benefit from the product or services you promote. You need to understand implicitly the value and benefits of those products or services. You may not be the most skilled and experienced at your company, or in your industry for that matter, but you can be the most prepared. If you develop a reputation for being prepared—that your ability to prepare for each opportunity exceeds that of your peers—it will only be a matter of time before success follows.

Here's an example of what not to do. I met with a web company that claimed to specialise in social media marketing, but a quick review of the strategy they had implemented for their own business revealed they were barely qualified to even talk about the subject. Cash flow aside, it is often a lack of credibility that cripples a business. No proven track record and limited relevant experience in a supplier are all risks for a potential customer—investing money in your product or service is too risky. To help combat this, you must demonstrate your competence at every opportunity. Dare to prepare! If you're a realtor, own your own properties—start as small as you need to. If this suburb really is the next boom town, why aren't you in this market already? Dare to prepare and speak from experience. If you're a web developer, show me a world class website and strategy—all that should cost is your own creativity, resources and some time. Mr Financial Planner, I want to know about your asset portfolio and the risks you took and overcame to achieve personal wealth. If you can't save yourself, don't expect others to pay you to save them.

Unlocking your inner game

Preparation is an activity but, more importantly, it's also a mindset. When you find yourself preparing for your next big pitch or planning a meeting with your manager for your performance review, ask yourself, 'Why should the person I am talking with trust and buy from me and believe in what I'm saying?' You then connect that response in your head to what you want to achieve.

If you're really honest, a sincere response to this question is often a slight pause, followed by a blank stare. Okay, I will ask this question in a slightly different way.

'Other than making money, why are you in business?' That question will invariably be greeted with another ponderous look, or it might trigger a passionate reply, such as, 'I just love helping people!' or 'I really enjoy the culture here, just look around us: you can almost smell the passion in the air!' *Eureka!* These insights, and others like them, are clues to help you to understand the 'why' for doing what you do, or desire to do. It also helps you to start to clarify why someone will ultimately buy from you. From here you can start to form your 'why frame', which shapes the initial step of your customer engagement process. This is the moment and place where all relevant communication should start or finish.

At my sales development company, *BOOM!*, we use an intelligent method for breaking down how salespeople communicate word by word and then aligning their communication to their customer's emotional drivers, that is, the things that really turn their customers on and influence their behaviour. If a word or statement doesn't support the customer's 'why', it's swiftly removed from their vocabulary or reframed in a more meaningful way and acutely aligned to the customer's needs or desires. Omit needless words, of course. Next is taking some time out to see things from the client perspective.

Activity: developing your 'why frame'

First, round up your teammates, especially those who have a role engaging and influencing customers. Fetch a whiteboard or an easel with butcher's paper and marker pens. If you don't have a board, then simply pin the paper to the wall. Next, elect a team leader to lead and facilitate the group discussion. The facilitator's objective is to write down all the key emotional drivers that relate to your most valuable customers. Namely, what are they fearful about when buying from your company or others in your industry? What frustrates the pants off them when it comes to your product, service or industry (this is always the longest list). And what do they really want and need from you, and why?

Think practically and think broadly. But most of all, be brutally honest. The output of this activity is to then drill down to the most critical insights and then craft and design your communication around the customer, not you. You will also need to cut out certain areas of focus to free up your time to zero in on communicating the right message to the right customers, more often. And remember, have fun with it!

It's also important to remember that if a potential customer contacts you, consider 'why' they have gone to the effort of seeking you out? Don't disregard this information. And don't make the error of assuming that every customer that initiates contact with you already has a compelling and resolved 'why' in their mind. It's always up to you to help them unlock and emphasise their 'why' in your initial sales conversation as you set the tone, build rapport and establish fit with the customer. Likewise, if you conduct outbound marketing activities, your success rates will dramatically improve when you demonstrate you have taken time to really think about your 'why' for calling by communicating your insight-driven and critical piece of information that moves the customer to a place of safe and purposeful action. Failure to do so will typically result in a swift and cold 'Goodbye!'. We will explore this concept more in chapter 2 when we discuss the Red Phone principle.

To see things in the seed, that is genius.

Lao Tzu, author of *Tao Te Ching*

What can we learn from a bushranger?

Ned Kelly was a shameless horse thief and bank robber, who admitted to gunning down policemen. The son of an Irish convict, Kelly became Australia's most infamous leader of a gang of Outlaws. There's much to learn from

Outlaws and the lengths they go to prepare for battle and fight for their cause. Getting things wrong could result in their paying the ultimate price or spending the rest of their life behind bars. Outlaws like Kelly communicate and survive through underground networks made up of like-minded people. They rely on trusted sources for their intelligence and information to aid them in their mission or project. What was most intriguing about Ned Kelly was his penchant for innovation, not just his iron will but also the iron armour he wore, concealed under his coat, in his last stand against police.

Kelly may not be a poster boy for moral purity, but he defied the rules, he became an innovator and game changer, and folk hero. The armour Kelly wore was half his body weight. During the siege at Glenrowan, in June 1880, all four members of the Kelly gang (Ned and Dan Kelly, Joe Byrne and Steve Hart) wore suits of armour made of plate metal. Kelly was an inventor. Body armour in Australia is not only outrageous given the rugged conditions, in this case it was absurdly heavy, making the energy required to wear it immense. But it was real genius. Kelly showed a capacity to think creatively and a willingness and resilience to fight for what he believed in, that is, the unjust and corrupt way the police operated and enforced the law of the land.

Genuine innovation can be game-changing. But only when you are genuinely prepared to go to all and extreme lengths to see your vision manifest. A strong measure of how committed you really are can be observed in the time and thought you invest in preparing for each battle. I'm not suggesting you become a rum swilling, bearded bandit and decorate yourself in heavy metal. I'm encouraging you to periodically take the time out with your colleagues to challenge what is not working and what is working, so it can be improved upon. Most importantly, think about how you can radically change your situation, environment or client outcomes. This is achieved not just by thinking outside the box, but by creating a completely new box.

I do not wish to give the order full force without giving timely warning but I am a widow's son outlawed and must be obeyed.

Ned Kelly, bushranger

De-risking your value proposition

You have to be prepared to take a risk or two to succeed. But don't expect your customers to have the same level of zest for risk-taking. Particularly when they know they will ultimately pay for it when the risk turns sour, or you, as the salesperson, under-deliver. For the most part, taking risks is a tense and uncomfortable experience for a customer. Each customer will have a different risk threshold: a level of perceived risk they are willing to move towards but never cross over. As sales professionals we can at times underestimate the inherent risks relating to what we sell. These risks can seem immaterial to us, but they can be debilitating for customers—particularly if we have never purchased a similar product or taken time out to assess the risks from the consumer's point of view.

Customers are cautious creatures and even more so when the economy is flat. This can be frustrating for both the vendor and customer. The customer laments, 'I really want to buy, but I just don't trust my ability to pay or receive the required value leverage, it's too risky.' And the salesperson grumbles, 'I know you need my help, but what else do I need to demonstrate to gain your trust?' These stalemates play out habitually in challenging markets. The best way to cut through the customer's fear is to remove all traces of perceived risk. In addition, provide them with critical information that takes them to a place of new knowledge and clarity. To really drive change, or change the customer's point of view, you will need to completely commit to your commercial cause and be willing to fight for it, because ultimately you're fighting for the customer. Giving up at the first sign of rejection from a customer tells them how committed you really are and it validates their lack of belief in you. When you apply the right de-risking strategy and communicate from a place of belief, the customer will be transformed from frozen and confused to willing and motivated.

Tips to leverage risk and help the customer see more value

- Reduce risk by demonstrating how much time and energy you have invested in preparation.

- Acknowledge the customer's risks and probe to evaluate the importance of each risk.

- Identify the most serious risks and introduce your new critical piece of information that helps them to overcome it and confidently move forward.

- Add more value by introducing added complimentary products or services (high perceived value/low cost) at the appropriate time.

- Share case studies or personal stories about how you or your customers successfully overcame similar risks and their related benefits.

- Offer longer payment terms that activate your product's value immediately.

- Always be empathetic, and remember it's much easier to give risk advice than to live the risk.

- Be willing to say 'no' if you genuinely feel the risk outweighs the value for the customer (trade the short-term for the long-term gain or credibility).

The risks will vary for each customer. Presuming the risks are only attached to losing money is folly. The investment side is always important, but it's not often the most significant risk. Be sure to consider how getting the purchase wrong will impact a customer's reputation; again draw reference to the insight you collated in the 'why frame' activity. Similarly, consider how a past negative experience as it relates to your company or industry may now be determining their behaviour and risk profile. Risk is powerful when you harness it correctly and help your customers see through it.

Why not go out on a limb? That's where the fruit is.

Mark Twain, American author and humourist

Hunt and herd your competition

The next step in your preparation is getting up close and personal with your competitors. Don't be scared: they won't bite. Hmm, some might, so proceed carefully. Sales is a contact sport and when it comes to competitors it should be full body contact! Most markets are saturated with competitors manoeuvring themselves in their most attractive guises to lure the affection of would-be customers. Competition serves the collective as merchants are kept on their toes. Customers are able to select a provider that best meets their needs or desires. Many businesspeople underestimate their competitors — pretending they don't exist or that what they do is somehow irrelevant or somehow inferior in comparison. Don't make that mistake.

By default, we often frame our competitors as the enemy. We have never met them, and don't have the desire to. If they're flying a flag with a different brand, they spell evil! This belief is not only ignorant, it's also limiting and ultimately self-defeating. Call me mad, but I recommend meeting with competitors periodically. Invite them for coffee or chat over the phone. Learn what they are up to. How do they communicate and what do they really stand for? What's their story and where are they headed? Are they arrogant and aloof, or polished or coarse? This is important information to know. Here's why: if you know what's really beneath your competitor's facade, it helps you understand how to position yourself in either a contrasting or a more meaningful light.

Understanding competitors

Competitors commonly fall into three distinct categories:

1 closed and aggressive

2 passive and indifferent

3 open and collaborative.

Misguided by tradition, we can be guilty of herding all competitors into category 1. Competitors in this class generally come from a place of fear and scarcity, and many are overtly self-righteous. You will be able to establish this when you make contact and receive no response or a negative retort. Leave these competitors to fester in their own ignorance, or hunt and destroy them—it's up to you. If you are willing to make the effort and initiate contact with competitors, you will find that most fall into category 2. These people are somewhat short-sighted, but they are rarely sinister. They are not competitors to think too much about or deal with strategically. Safely share your innermost secrets with them: they won't use them against you. They are frequently content and quite happy where they are in the pecking order.

Category 3 is not only a characterisation, it's a way of being. Usually competitors in this group have realised there is enough for everyone. They also know how competition serves them and their customers. My own research over the past 10 years reveals that less than 10 per cent of companies fall into this category. Most of the others aren't capable of understanding how collaborating and sharing knowledge with a perceived enemy can serve them and others. Doctors and medical specialists are skilled proponents of this approach. They don't take on a procedure if it's not their area of expertise and habitually refer patients to someone more qualified. What's more, they regularly seek expert counsel from other specialists. Their resolve is to always create the right outcome for the patient. People's health and lives are at stake. What a powerful way of operating. Aren't your customers that important? If not, they should be.

I regularly make contact with competitors, and when appropriate refer business to them. I have learned some interesting things from some of them, and from others I have learned what not to do. Establishing connections with competitors in different markets or geographic regions you're not active in also enables you to cross-pollinate best practice and leverage intellectual property (IP); ultimately this mutually enhances knowledge and capability and serves the best interests of customers.

Time for action!

I encourage you to make contact with no fewer than three key competitors you respect, and ask for a catch-up over the phone or, better, in person. When you meet, come from a place of contribution, commonality and, if possible, try to help them in some way. You will invariably find your competitors are facing the same challenges as you, and you have a lot more in common with them than you think. Going into a new business meeting armed with fresh insights and intelligence about your competitors and how you can provide a contrasting or superior offer to them is not only the act of a virtuous salesperson but a sign of a person who has come prepared.

I destroy my enemies when I make them my friend.

Abraham Lincoln, 16th US President

The Fat Duck: Heston Blumenthal

Preparation extremist Heston Blumenthal is an English chef. This culinary maestro makes his dishes sing to an unfamiliar tune. He is entirely self-taught and had never had a paying job as a chef until he opened his own restaurant, The Fat Duck. Blumenthal is one of only three British chefs to have received three Michelin stars.

What you will notice about Heston if you flick onto his many celebrated television shows, such as *Heston's Feasts*, is how much effort and thought he invests in creating his astonishingly innovative and outrageous dishes. Each dish, dripping with intense flavour, is formulated by a process he applies to theme his dishes to a historic period. You won't just see Heston wielding a deathly meat clever, you will more frequently observe him fiddling with test tubes as dry ice whooshes into the ceiling fans. Heston has made his mark not just by creating a world-class menu: he transforms the molecular structure of food so it looks like one thing and tastes like another. Exotic pig stomach and truffle mimics a lush navel orange you would pluck straight off a tree. Or how about some worm pizza?

Blumenthal serves worm pizza to kids in hospital. He believes the worms are loaded with protein and can bring a healthy spice and improvement to the hospital menu. Others may think differently, but I am not sure it would make much difference. This guy was brought in to make a difference and that is what he is doing. Blumenthal spends hours every week researching and testing new recipes in his elaborate kitchen-cum-science lab. Many dishes don't fly, but that doesn't deter him, and the ones that do leave his patrons gobsmacked. He is a masterful chef who sees his craft as more than cooking: for him, it's about creating a completely new dining experience and taking his patrons on a culinary adventure. Every dish is an opportunity for Heston to defy the rules, drive change and deliver more, and set new standards of excellence.

It was quite a challenge to make people eat crab ice-cream.

Heston Blumenthal, chef

Attack of the time-wasters

Every year your sales target mysteriously spikes up. It's as if the target fairy sneaks into the CFO's bedroom on 30 June at the stroke of midnight and sprinkles the new target underneath his pillow. Damn your fairy: another 10 per cent increase—why? With no rhyme, reason or justification, that's just how it is, so it's best you prepare for it.

Costs go up? Of course they do. Competition increases? You bet. Every year you are asked to achieve more but you aren't provided with any additional time or resources. To hit your new target each year, you need to learn how to do more with less. Here's how—not only do you need to be more efficient and spend more time on high-value activities, you must, without hesitation, attack the time-wasters before they attack you!

Such seductive creatures they are! But don't be fooled by their allure: their impact on your business is costly and must be eradicated immediately. Make no mistake: time-wasters are the enemy! Forget about your competitors for a moment—they're the least of your concerns. Particularly, when you are chasing your tail or failing to spend your valuable time on core tasks that deliver the greatest level of output, and the business is being eaten alive at both ends. Every salesperson is forced to deal regularly with time-wasters, if not daily: time-wasters talk too much, ask too many questions, and fail to make a decision, but keep contacting you for more free information. So why is this type of customer still so vexing and alluring to most sales professionals? Immature salespeople rarely possess the skills and confidence to successfully deal with time-wasters: they will often follow a standard process, or no process, that applies to all, rather than adapting their approach and focusing on the right customers.

More experienced sales professionals can fall victim to their own egos. Believing in their own hype and overestimating their ability to sell anything to anyone—they broaden their focus, look for short cuts, and get lazy. Others are simply desperate. They live in hope, ignoring their intuition and pouring their precious time into a vacuum.

To overcome time-wasters, as a sales leader you need to get deadly serious about educating and training the right salespeople to work according to a tested and targeted sales process and adapt it when necessary. As a salesperson, simply read on. Salespeople in any company, irrespective of industry, must learn to be confident and comfortable saying 'no'. You must do the following:

- Say 'no' to customers who are not defined as enablers, critical influencers or decision makers—see the section on the Red Phone on pages 32–38 for more information on this concept.

- Say 'no' to companies or people who are way outside your target market—review your 'why frame' and the people and companies you are most qualified to help.

- Say 'no' to customers that take you beyond the parameters of what you know works.

- Say 'no' to demanding, self-righteous and unprofitable customers.

- Say 'no' to salespeople who give managers endless excuses for underperformance.

- Say 'no' to sales managers who won't get their hands dirty when it's required.

'No' is such a purposeful word when you apply it to time-wasters with sincerity. The best defence is attack. Get on the front foot by mapping your stakeholders (an activity we will explore in the next chapter) and by being crystal clear on what customers you can successfully contribute most to. The rest can go to your competitors or spend their time filling someone else's vacuum.

> *We must use time wisely and forever realise that the time is always ripe to do right.*
>
> Nelson Mandela,
> anti-apartheid and civil rights leader

Choose a mentor wisely

If you want to change the game you will need a strong support network. Working with a mentor is one of most productive things you can do for yourself in life and in business. It is also a key element in your preparation. Being able to share your fears and frustrations, desires and aspirations with someone you trust and respect, in a safe environment, is invaluable. I have only one rule of thumb when it comes to working with a mentor—choose them wisely. Over the years I have had several mentors. The mentors who haven't contributed any lasting value have always been what I call wounded bulls, or people who project an image of success but who are really concealing a personal agenda. Unfortunately, I met a couple of wounded bulls early in my career who not only gave me poor advice, but also vanished when I most needed help.

I have also been fortunate enough to have had a mentor in my life who was literally life-changing. He was Big Kev (Kevin McQuay), and for those who don't live in Australia, he was one of Australia's most flamboyant TV salesmen. He built a multimillion-dollar cleaning-product company, listed it on the Australian Securities Exchange (ASX) and became a household name. Big in personality and size, Kev cut a figure that even the most self-assured of silverback gorillas would be proud of. Kev was one of a kind. He was completely original and boldly authentic, decorating himself in outrageously bright silk shirts. He had quite a wit and a tongue so sharp it could cut you to pieces at 20 paces. Big Kev sadly passed away a number of years ago, but it's clear to me that today my life is vastly more colourful and richer because of him. We spent hours not only drinking and frequenting ritzy restaurants (his favourite pastime), but also immersed in discussions about life and business. Invaluable insights I still carry with me.

No matter what you've been through in life or are yet to endure, someone else has been there before you. A valuable mentor has been there, so they will also help you navigate the murky fog of ambiguity and offer practical advice to help you get towards your destination, wherever that may be. Your customer should consider you, in part, a mentor too. Why wouldn't they? After all, you are the expert at what you do. They rely on you.

A mentor can be used to develop most areas in business, but will be particularly useful in planning and developing areas that are not your natural strong suit. You don't need to meet your mentor in person every day or week: the arrangement can simply be ad hoc, for when you need advice or on the fly. Just remember a mentor's time is invaluable and they are often in demand, so don't abuse their time and generosity. And always, without compromise, offer to help your mentor in some way in return if you can. Just because they are successful doesn't mean they don't need help too.

Mentors are all around us: in my experience they have always materialised through people that I know and trust, making them a safer bet, but not guaranteed. Just remember to always be wary of a wounded bull. Working with a mentor that you don't know very well can be perilous, so proceed cautiously and do your due diligence. This principle also applies if your mentor is charging a fee for their time. In my experience successful mentors are older, but that's not always the case; depending on their areas of skill, and level of experience and industry, they could indeed be younger. And not all successful people are effective mentors; this will depend on their natural instinct for coaching. Working with a mentor shouldn't cost you more than a coffee or odd lunch here and there, but if you find the right one, your small investment could pay off handsomely.

You need to be surrounded by good advisers, but you also have to trust your instincts.

Chris Hughes, co-founder of Facebook

Rules and records are made to be broken

Each generation strives to be more than their ancestors: more opulent, more enlightened, more successful, smarter, faster! To achieve this you will need to overcome ignorance, abolish inhibiting beliefs, and embrace and harness change. This path can be risky, but ultimately, it will serve you by moving you forward and upward. To evolve, your own records need to be broken and new rules established. We all live in a world of flux and ceaseless movement, and if you're standing still, in reality, you're moving backwards.

Genuine game-changing innovation can be challenging to achieve, because initially only you believe in it. Without others buying into your vision, who will embrace and run with it? Not many—which usually spells the death of a great idea or grand ideal. True innovators live on the edge, blazing away with original ideas and brazen beliefs. To defy a long-held record or tradition set by others, you will need a stomach full of courage, a thick skin and unyielding commitment to your cause. Never succumb to other people's ignorance or take unconstructive feedback as a reason to quit your dream. Guard it with your life. Fight for it. You are unstoppable when your vision sings to your determination and inspires you to work through adversity. Keep driving! Sticking your neck out is not for the faint hearted, especially if what you believe in runs contrary to the majority. Be prepared to work. Be prepared to stick. Take on feedback, but don't listen to the naysayers.

At some point, much of what you believe in and take for granted today will evolve or change, so be open to change. Why not drive it? But what shouldn't change are your values, your self-belief and desire keep on improving. And if you genuinely believe something needs to be broken—smash it! The default setting for most people is to under-prepare. Not surprisingly, these are people who are only scratching the surface of their full potential. Whenever I speak with an audience, large or small, a single glaring area for improvement is always apparent. I recall speaking to an audience of more than 200 sales consultants. I quizzed them to each raise their hand if they believed they could prepare more effectively on a day-to-day basis? In a nanosecond 200 hands reached for the sky in unison. 'Hallelujah!' I celebrated. Awareness is one thing, but taking action is quite another. Dare to prepare!

Luck is preparation meeting opportunity.

Oprah Winfrey, media mogul and philanthropist

☞ Action points ☜

- Develop your 'why frame' with teammates to craft and align your communication to your customers and their emotional drivers.

- Establish your competitor profiles—closed and aggressive, passive and indifferent or open and collaborative—to learn more about them and develop strategies to deal with them.

- Attack your time-wasters before they attack you. Just say no! Get clear about who your high-value customers are, and free up your time to focus on and find more of them.

- The most successful salespeople are always the best prepared. Dare to prepare!

CHAPTER 2

INSPIRE WITH WORDS AND ACTIONS

A superior man is modest in his speech, but exceeds in his actions.

Confucius, Chinese philosopher

Now we are prepared, let's get some forward movement, because you are measured by your actions above all else. The sharpness of a salesperson's tongue and their ability to communicate with passion and conviction go a long way towards their success. Yet, words play only a minor role in the influence equation. What you say, and how you say it, along with your corresponding actions, determine just how believable and trustworthy you, the salesperson, really are.

Customers wanted ~~dead or~~ alive

An age-old question that still baffles too many businesspeople is whether the customer is always right. How you or your team members ponder this question and answer it will provide valuable insights into how your company values and treats its customers.

Is the customer always right? Let me explore this topic, before I give a definite answer. Outlaws carefully challenge their customers to drive change and reframe the way they see things. In doing so they take their customers beyond their comfort zone, provided of course that shift serves them: this is the mark of a virtuous salesperson. In contrast, less savvy salespeople damage their employer's brand by dismissing a valuable customer's problem or, worse, turning it into a confrontation. Conclusion: the customer is always right! Translation: the customer and their unique needs and challenges matter.

Does that mean you obey every customer demand and let them lead your process? Of course not, but it does mean you start with the customer's view in mind, empathise with it—don't dismiss it—then add colour and shade by introducing new insights and perspectives to help them see things differently. Pushing back at a customer aggressively is called arrogance—some would also say ignorance. In contrast, genuinely listening and empathising when a client expresses their dissatisfaction and then guiding the situation towards a positive outcome is a sign of genuine wisdom. When you understand that the customer's feelings are primary and you remove your ego from the sales conversation—and from confronting conversations—the way you are experienced will shift from a place of ignorance to a place of pure clarity and confidence. Fighting small meaningless battles every day is not only emotionally draining, it's unendearing. It also suggests you're missing opportunities to learn about and strengthen your customer relationships. When you really listen, particularly when a customer laments their frustrations, you become humble, and a willingness to take constructive feedback on board shows you care. There's no better gesture you can offer a customer.

Perhaps it is better to be irresponsible and right,
than to be responsible and wrong.

Winston Churchill, wartime Prime Minister
of the United Kingdom

Your most demanding customers are nearly always your greatest teachers. They will draw attention to your flaws and misgivings in fine detail. If you fail to lower your guard and integrate their relevant input you will limit your ability to expand your skills and capabilities.

'All buyers are liars' is another old chestnut. Translation: customers will do and say anything to get the best deal for themselves. And rightly so, so don't make it too hard for them. Some customers will bend the truth, but usually for a valid reason. To counter this, design a transparent process that provides all parties with the right information to make the right decision and move the conversation forward. (We will explore this in more detail in chapter 4.) If your customers are still demonstrating deceptive behaviour, take that as a cue to rethink your strategy or tweak your communication style. Customers are not the enemy: your success relies on them. Consider your customers as part of your extended family—you may not agree with them from time to time, but you always care about their best interests.

A modern gold rush

The past decade has witnessed a communications revolution. We are being influenced by an array of new media. There is no denying the internet has changed the way we all live and conduct business. Today, social media sites are ingrained into our communities. The world has gone app mad—me included. Facebook, now valued in the scores of billions, is staking its claim as a social communications pillar, and in doing so setting a fresh tone for the way we interact and engage with one another and our customers. Facebook has rapidly eroded market share from fledgling global social networking site MySpace, now a music platform enduring a slow and painful death. A plethora of offshoots have sprung up—from the practical, such as photo-sharing platform Instagram, to a bizarre social site that connects would be suitors to cheating partners. Twitter is another social site to hit it big. What's clever about Twitter's model is that it has taken Facebook's most popular feature, the update, refined it and then built a phenomenal business from it. Think about how you can implement a similar approach with some of your competitors, namely those you define as closed and aggressive.

I do still question the long-term value of these so-called social sites, other than to distract us from what is real and important in the world. They also provide yet another channel for opportunistic people to try to sell something to people who probably don't need or even want it. Let's be honest: how many friends and followers do you really have on Facebook? Facebook should change its definition of Friends to Prospects and Twitter should change 'Follow' to 'I want to sell you something'.

The real power of social media is directed more towards business to consumer (B2C) markets. Much like radio, TV and direct marketing, social media is a mass market channel. Social networking sites may start off as a great idea with grand ideals, but human beings, the most cunning of all species, soon work out how to leverage these platforms to their own advantage. Facebook is now a revenue-generating machine, yet I'm still underwhelmed by the number of businesses that are gaining any real traction from Facebook's paid advertising platform. Facebook is cashing in regardless. The internet offers exceptional benefits, because it's quick and easy, saves us time and money, and provides unprecedented access to information, which also gives transparency and accountability. But don't get too caught up in it. And don't use it as your only means of engaging people or abuse it as channel to blatantly sell something.

Don't get too distracted by the internet and don't let it distract you from what is truly important to you—like developing real relationships with real people. Do you want your kids to grow up thinking that the best way to communicate is through a chat room or social networking site? Sadly this is becoming the reality, so take heed now. Fresh in my mind is an experience I had at a train station. As I scanned the terminal I saw most people with their heads down fiddling with their smart phones, not aware of what was going on around them. I say harness the internet and social channels to their full potential, but keep your head up, always.

The age of social enlightenment

Most of the hype in social media is aimed at page promotion, and getting liked and followed. One area that often escapes mainstream attention is the incredible platform that social media provides to acquire more personal information about people that you can then apply in a meaningful way. To inspire with words and actions you will need to genuinely make the effort to get to know your customers as people, not just dollar signs. They may not want to get to know you better, and that's okay, but there is no harm in making the effort. I connect with most of my key clients and contacts in social networks, because I want to learn more about them. For example, Facebook serves up details such as the names of family members and favourite family activities, as well as the restaurants they frequent, sporting teams they support and even where they went to school and with whom.

Who needs a private detective?

Profiles on professional site LinkedIn provide information about a client's network and, if someone you know is connected to them, you can quickly ask them for some insights. Never before could we access this type of information about someone without developing a direct relationship with them. The sceptics may say this development has dangerous ramifications and that enhanced transparency will lead to an increase in deceptive behaviour. I tend to agree, but like anything in life, the devil dwells in extremes. The information people display in this medium is meaningful to them, so make it meaningful to you. Don't use personal details to manipulate, use them to communicate in a way that demonstrates a genuine interest in your customers as people instead of potential transactions. Common sense should always prevail: respect the boundaries of others and don't be too quick to judge. Often a public face is what people want you to see, which can be misleading. Interestingly, the more you know about your customers, the less you will need to sell to them.

Fast is fine, but accuracy is everything.

Wyatt Earp, 19th century American law enforcer

Waving the pirate flag: Steve Jobs

The late, great Steve Jobs was the world's best salesperson. How can I make a statement like that with so much conviction and not bat an eyelid? It's not because Jobs built a billion-dollar brand that redefined how we communicate and consume music. It's not because he had a rock-star persona and customers saw him more like their fearless leader than a tech entrepreneur. It's not because he was fired from his company and then came back a decade later fiercer than ever. It's for one reason: he packed out stadiums to present his latest products. Can you think of anyone else who has achieved this feat? Certainly no-one quite like Jobs. His presentations are the stuff of legend. Customers lined up along the footpath, not unlike fervent football fans queuing in the cold with ticket clutched in hand in anticipation of the big game.

Like lots of Apple things, Jobs didn't invent the keynote address. But, again like a lot of Apple things, he popularised a certain form of it: a dynamic (yet minimalist) show that saw him as the ringmaster in a circus of products, features and apps, punctuated heavily with superlatives and self-congratulation. It's a style that has been emulated and spoofed time and again. One of the things Apple fans looked forward to most in a Jobs keynote address was 'One more thing,' the surprise item he would roll out just as it looked like he was wrapping up. Jobs introduced such notable products as the Apple AirPort, iPod Shuffle and MacBook Air with this gimmick.

The best was at the Macworld convention in 2007. 'Every once in a while a revolutionary product comes along that changes everything.' With those words, Steve Jobs introduced the first Apple iPhone.

In the early days Apple chose as an enemy the market leader of the day, Big Blue, better known as IBM, the world's largest manufacturer of computer technology. Big Blue staff dressed in suits, so to challenge this stiff corporate image, the Apple team dressed in sneakers, t-shirts and jeans. Jobs seemed to see the future and had a clear vision of what he wanted the Apple brand to represent. In an industry dominated by one player, Apple had to be different to succeed, hence their famous tagline 'Think Different', which embodies and communicates the Outlaw spirit.

Elements of style

William Strunk's classic work on the rules of usage in English, *The Elements of Style*, has helped writers like me to better understand the fundamentals of fluent and concise writing. Strunk's golden and timeless key principle, 'Omit needless words', is a simple and elegant rule often disregarded in both written and verbal communication. Most salespeople have a natural tendency to over-communicate—we are too quick to fill the empty space in the conversation with words that could be described as insipid banter. Most experienced salespeople can relate to having a meeting with someone who gives them nothing but a blank stare and one-word responses. Unlike preparation, in which more is indeed more, when it comes to communication, less is often more.

An Outlaw, by definition, is an outward projection as opposed to an inward and self-directed projection. No skill demonstrates this more than listening. When it comes to listening, Outlaws are ferocious in being able to absorb information, and then adapt and tailor the messages to the needs and communication preferences of the customer. Research shows that versatile salespeople can be up to 50 per cent more effective than those who demonstrate no versatility in this area. Demonstrating the skills to recognise the customer's communication preferences, and to adapt your own approach to more directly meet those preferences, has proven to be a key to the success of the sales conversation. When people say that they connect with someone, they are referring to the similarity of their communication styles. We feel more comfortable with, and often trust, people who like to communicate in a similar manner to ourselves; who talk at a similar pace and in a similar tonality; who use a similar level of gesture; who are not too pushy and like to get to know us at about the same pace we are willing to share our personal information.

Aligning communication

Social and psychological research indicates that people are divided equally across four primary social styles: director, socialiser, relater and thinker. Figure 2.1 (adapted from the model by Virginia Satir, American child psychotherapist and social worker) shows the four most common communication styles and their relevant focus. Keeping in mind that we all may at times demonstrate the characteristic of each quadrant, by and large all people will have a natural default setting they are more comfortable and confident in over others.

Figure 2.1: the four communication styles

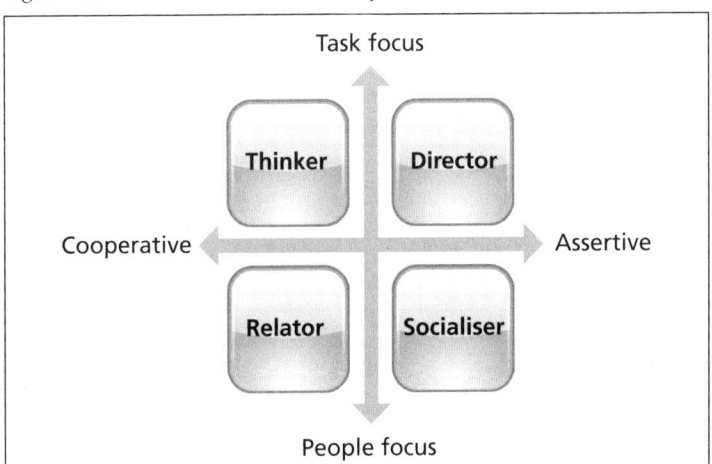

You will find common themes appear if you integrate these profiles into your Arc of Influence, a simple tool for identifying time-wasters, enablers, critical influencers and decision makers (we explore this concept later in this chapter when we talk about the Red Phone). For example, if the decision maker is a CFO, they are likely to have a thinker or a thinker/director profile. Likewise, if your critical influencers are HR managers, they will mostly be relaters, given the people focus of their jobs. Understanding customers' social style will help you tailor your approach, even before you have met or spoken with them. Understanding these characteristics helps you establish their profile and make educated assumptions about their potential challenges or requirements, which will help you in your preparation and your ability to make a positive and impactful first impression. You will also pick up clues when you speak with them, helping you to further tailor your message. Because each style represents about 25 per cent of our customers, most salespeople will only naturally connect with one out of every four customers. Most of a salesperson's sales will tend to come from the customers they naturally relate to. Salespeople who are able to recognise the styles and preferences of their customers, and, more importantly, adapt their natural style to minimise the differences between themselves and their customers, are more likely to be able to connect with the other 75 per cent of their customers. Sales success will increase, because it is easier to sell to customers with whom we connect.

Let's move on now from verbal communication to the less impactful use of email to engage and influence customers.

The real cost of spam

Email is so quick and easy, but it's too easily abused. You only get one shot to make a positive first impression. When you are using outbound marketing there is always a fine line between persistence and harassment. Business is tougher today than it was a decade ago, and customers are less loyal than they once were. They have their guards up, making it harder to engage with customers and lead them through your sales conversation. As a trusted adviser, you also need to respect your customer's right to privacy and take every communication channel seriously. Never compromise the integrity of your communication or brand reputation for the promise of a few quick and easy wins. This leads us to email marketing and spam—the other version of spam is cheap processed meat. The parallels are not lost on me.

Some people believe that it's acceptable and effective to bombard customers with self-focused marketing jargon. They also believe it's free and easy to send emails, so they blast them out hundreds, and even thousands, at a time to unsuspecting recipients, hoping that a tiny percentage will either buy now or buy something, anything, downstream. This approach may appear to be relatively free and easy, even cost-effective, but there are implicit and dangerous costs associated with abusing it. As a business owner, whenever I receive an email I'm usually expecting to find something of significant value to me in my inbox—like a response from a customer, a request for my services or a message from a friend. When I get spammed, I never read it—ever. In fact, my reflex is now so instinctive that I hit the delete button without hesitation! So, if you are serious about engaging me in a meaningful way, understand that spam, much like thoughtless cold-calling, is only going to aggravate me and train me to ignore you.

You will push away potential customers if you abuse email. By pushing email in your sales conversation, you alienate customers who simply need more time and space to consider their response. Sending an email every second day until you get a response from a customer is as thoughtless as it is irritating. Bombarding mailing lists with emails containing content about you that's neither relevant nor valuable is futile. If you're relying on this approach as a lead generation tool, I suggest you feed the spam to the dog (Fluffy probably won't eat it either) and then keep reading. By all means harness the benefits of email, but make sure you're not abusing it or your customers simply because you can.

Buy in before you sell in

Unlike spam, clear and succinct communication via email to people who know or trust you is effective. However, if you need to achieve something of critical importance, you will still pick up the telephone as the preferred mode of communication. This makes the phone, despite the internet, still the single most powerful communication tool on hand for a salesperson, other than face-to-face contact.

Words are meaningless without emotion, and emotions, like body language, are challenging to express and digest over the phone, especially when you are speaking with a stranger and expecting them to believe you and be influenced enough to want to follow you. Remember, over 50 per cent of all communication is achieved through non-verbal cues, such as facial expression, gesture and posture. That means that most cold-callers, even the really high-performers, are still limited by phone-related challenges. Be mindful, if you are choosing the telephone as your initial point of contact and as an introduction to a potential customer, that you need to communicate a critical piece of information in a way that moves them to a point of action, or there is a form of consequence if they don't take action. This has to be something real—very real. Imposters need not read any further: your tricks are of little value here.

Don't make a direct call to a stranger unless you are buying-in with your customer's objective first. Here's why. When a person picks up the phone they are expecting to hear someone they know or a person who is going to add value for them, like a potential customer looking to buy, so don't disappoint. Make your direct call as a trusted adviser or a genuine buyer, or don't call at all.

You have to demonstrate that you are interested to be more interesting, so you don't get the too-frequently heard response from a high-potential prospect: 'Sorry, I'm not interested, goodbye!' What the customer is really saying is, 'You have not demonstrated a genuine interest in me or my best interests and for that reason, I'm not interested in listening to what you have to say.'

For too many companies buying-in is too hard. They just don't prepare and make the effort to meet their clients or demonstrate the desire to develop meaningful conversations with customers. The dialogue is all about themselves and little else. Before you make your next call, ask yourself: am I genuinely calling because I am interested in contributing to someone in a positive way? Or am I simply calling to push my own agenda and make a sale to get paid?

The original Red Phone

Leaders of nations first did it. Military generals do it. Even high-powered CEOs do it. Just like you and me, when they need something of critical importance actioned or addressed, they pick up the Red Phone and make a direct call to the person who can most influence what they need to achieve. The original Red Phone was a direct line between Washington and Moscow during the Cold War. It was a direct line that could connect the two heads of state for critical discussions. Many decades on our world is now vastly more connected than ever before, yet cutting through to influencers and decision makers and getting them to take you seriously is harder than ever. We are all far too busy and well informed to indulge a self-focused stranger blatantly trying to sell us something over the phone. Countless past negative experiences have trained us to know better. However, the phone is still a powerful tool if you know how to utilise its qualities correctly.

Cold-calling is dead, but the Red Phone is alive and well

Yes, sadly, the rumours are true. I'm here to tell you that cold-calling is dead. He passed away peacefully in his sleep. God bless. He was old, frail and weak, his best days behind him, but his passing was painless. He enjoyed a long and fruitful life, but time catches up with all of us, things change and life goes on. RIP cold-calling.

What once served salespeople admirably is now an old rusty antiquated technique that does little more than waste time and energy, while offering the recipient nothing. Unlike cold-calling that typically requires minimal effort, just collating a database and hitting the phone until your conscience catches up with you, the Red Phone call requires thorough planning, a structure, investing time to determine why you are calling, having a depth of knowledge about whom you are calling, and knowing how your words and actions will inspire the recipient to action. Cold-calling is a numbers game, and an exhausting one at that. In contrast, applying the Red Phone is about quality not quantity of calls. One successful Red Phone call can be a game changer and set off a cascading effect that transforms your year or maybe even your career.

Red Phone calls are big, bold calls to influential people that can genuinely help you and dramatically impact your business. They are calls to people you can impact and contribute to in a big way. Let's now explore the Arc of Influence (see figure 2.2) to help you map and target your communication for your Red Phone calls.

Figure 2.2: the Arc of Influence

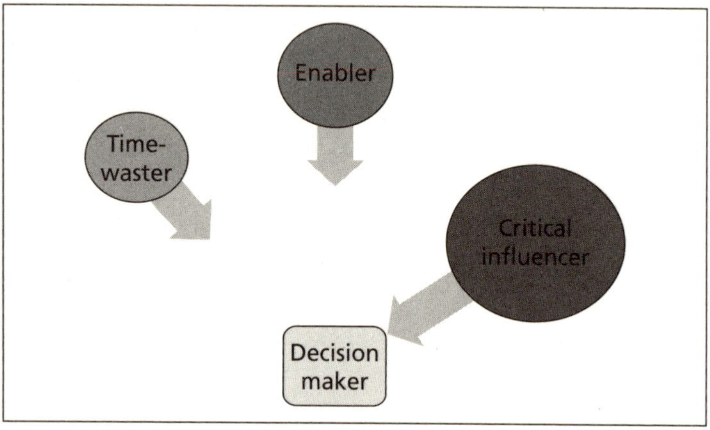

The Arc of Influence

There are four categories of customer in the Arc of Influence:

- *Time-waster.* These people are the enemy. Time-wasters will devour your valuable time, and leave you high and dry. These customers must be avoided or identified quickly and swiftly dealt with. Send them to your competitors.

- *Enabler.* These are people who cannot direct you to opportunities. They don't directly influence the decision to buy from you, but they have access to people who can. They are connectors and it is useful to cultivate relationships with these people.

- *Critical influencer.* You will see that this is the largest balloon, symbolising the relevance and the importance to you of the critical influencer. These people are the ones who cast the most influential vote as it relates to what you sell and do. These people influence the decision makers, making them essentially the 'decision makers'. They might not sign the cheques, but they are very active in the evaluation process and are in in most cases in the driver's seat. Here's why.

- *Decision maker.* This category is typically where most salespeople aim their communication. The first rule of the Red Phone is never cold-call a decision maker. They may sign the cheques, but they are rarely the sole influence on the decision and rarely make the buying decision themselves. Connecting to the decision maker through an established and credible relationship warms up the decision maker. This is best achieved by connecting via an enabler and then a critical influencer. If you pitch directly to the decision maker they will invariably take your proposal to a trusted adviser—and you won't have a relationship or credibility with the people who are really influencing the buying decision.

Today more and more buying decisions are being made through consensus. We collaborate and call on the insights and experience of trusted advisers to help us navigate our way through a complex and potentially prickly buying process. Furthermore, the decision maker requires buy-in to ensure all the parties involved once the purchase is made are invested in it, and also to hedge risk just in case things don't go to plan or, worse, go belly up. It is really important for salespeople to understand who the decision maker is and who the critical influencers are. They can vary from industry to industry, but there will also be consistencies you can understand to help you get clearer on your Arc of Influence. Your job as a salesperson is to identify the four profiles as early as possible so you can guide the sales conversation in the right direction.

To sum up: time-wasters are the enemy, cut through them quickly and dismiss or handball them to your competitors. Enablers are the people around you who connect you to opportunities and critical influencers. They have access to your target market through their personal or professional networks. If they connect you to a decision maker, be quick to identify the critical influencer and shift an area of your focus to them in a way that empowers the decision maker and demonstrates their need for consensus and buy-in without dismissing their authority.

Focus most of your time on understanding, getting to know, and building and nurturing relationships with critical influencers. These are the stakeholders who have the greatest impact and contribution to you achieving your goals. They help activate your success. Decision makers are important, so incorporate all their input and don't treat them as secondary to the critical influencer. And remember, never cold-call a decision maker. They are too time-poor to take a call or marketing email from a self-focused stranger. Don't insult them by thinking you can just walk off the street and sell them something. If only it was that simple. If you know who they are, your first step is to connect to the critical influencer via the enabler, or connect with the critical influencer directly.

True information does good.

Julian Assange, founder of WikiLeaks

The C Strategy

Your Red Phone call should consist of four critical elements that you target specifically at your critical influencer, once you have identified them. This method is called the C Strategy and figure 2.3 shows the step-by-step process.

Figure 2.3: the C Strategy for Red Phone calls

Critical influencer	✓ Never cold-call a decision maker. ✓ Map your Arc of Influence. ✓ Develop strategies to connect.
Confidence	✓ Do your research; acquire expertise. ✓ Activate a high performance state (HiPer). ✓ Nail the opening.
Credibility	✓ Transfer critical information quickly. ✓ Reveal your source and expertise. ✓ Add value or insights for buy-in and engagement.
Call to action	✓ Communicate a clear path to outcome. ✓ Gain the right to proceed and take control. ✓ Align the next step with your sales process.

The fourth and final element of the C Strategy, the call to action, should be aligned with the first step of your sales process. As you gain momentum, you then add shade and colour, and have some real fun with it. Most telephone tactics are little more than careless pleas for help from desperate salespeople who haven't worked out a meaningful approach to engage new customers. In contrast, the Red Phone is a masterful sales technique that will make a difference to how you proactively source and engage new customers.

Tips to master the Red Phone

- Never cold-call a decision maker. They are too time-poor and important. The buck stops with them, so once they say no, you will rarely get another chance to pitch.

- Understand your customers by working out who really influences the decision to buy from you and why (map and define your critical influencers and decision makers and their emotional drivers in fine detail).

- Embrace the age of social networks—tap into your network of connections, and use relevant media and social networks to source vital intelligence about your critical influencers.

- Who influences your critical influencer? Taking an indirect approach, before going direct, can be a smart approach and will pay dividends.

- Don't be intimidated when calling: instead, dare to prepare. Do your research—this could take not only hours, but even weeks.

- Make each call with at least one piece of critical information that empowers and educates your influencer in a new way—think of a fire chief calling local residents to evacuate. The message is clear: they come from a place of credibility and there is a strong call to action, and a consequence for inaction.

- Be credible and communicate from a place of commonality and expertise.

- Clearly communicate the outcome, and in doing so map out a path, establish buy-in and gain the right to proceed.

Apply only a few of these methods and you will be miles ahead of your average cold-caller.

How to get that big promotion

Influencing your sales manager isn't too dissimilar to how you influence your customers. If you dare to scale the slippery pole of success you will need to change your attitude and how you view yourself. In short, you will need to increase the value of your personal stock. Start taking your personal brand seriously (we will explore this in more detail in chapter 3 on personality). This will mean investing in and believing more in yourself.

What do a doctor, politician, priest and CEO all have in common? As people they are all defined by their title. What makes these titles, and others like them, so distinctive is not necessarily the person behind the title, but rather the perception and identity the title projects to others. The social expectations on a doctor are vastly different from those on a CEO. Every formal title brings with it a distinct meaning, yet all carry an expectation that marks the recipient and determines their actions and behaviour.

Does a job title mean someone is worthy of it, or less valuable because their title is seen as inferior to another's? Of course not, but the way a person demonstrates the responsibilities of their title can play a key role in what they achieve and how they are perceived by peers, their manager or their customers.

To achieve more you don't necessarily have to expect more from others, but you do need to expect more from yourself. You don't always need external encouragement to succeed, but your own expectations are critical. When you raise the bar and strive harder for the right reasons, you change into a person who defines their title and is deserving of that next big promotion.

Life is largely a matter of expectation.

Horace, ancient Roman poet

Reach for the stars: Jim Stynes

Jim Stynes, former AFL legend and founder of Reach, an organisation focused on helping young people, is an example of someone who inspired others with his words and actions. Stynes was as gangly as he was ferocious on the field. His ferocity to compete and win didn't end when he hung up his boots: he went on to co-found the Reach Foundation. Stynes passed away in 2012 after a courageous battle with cancer, but his inspiring legacy lives on through the thousands of teenagers that Reach empowers every year.

Reach was born from Styne's desire to inspire every young person to believe in themselves and get the most out of life. As someone who has worked with Reach as a mentor, as has my beautiful fiancée Kellie, I have seen the benefits of this extraordinary organisation up close and how it changes the lives of teenagers and contributes to society. It's not just the teenagers who benefit — we all do.

Reach provides preventive programs for more than 60 000 young Australians, aged 10–18, every year, within and outside the school system, and extending to over 580 schools and communities across the country. Anyone who wants to improve their self-confidence and get more from life is welcomed at Reach.

By creating safe spaces and positive peer group experiences, Reach provides an environment where young people can truly discover who they are. Its programs encourage young people to develop trust and openness, feel comfortable enough to express their concerns, discuss their aspirations and recognise that they're not alone. We know that self-belief is necessary for anyone to realise their potential and thrive, which is what makes Reach so special. Reach will never be on the *Fortune* 500 list, but what the organisation and its volunteers contribute to society is almost impossible to measure. RIP Jim, you will be missed.

Why sales managers are fast becoming redundant

If you're a sales manager your success is intrinsically linked to your team members believing in you and then following your lead. Telling your team how things should be done is impotent in comparison with communicating the path and then leading them by your actions. The days of micromanaging and demanding results from your team, like cold-calling, are well and truly over. Equally, support for salespeople can be overrated. In fact, I commonly see salespeople being over-supported. They are provided with everything from an encouraging manager, helpful resources to draw on, regular marketing initiatives and a generous salary, but still they underperform. There is a lot to be said for not hiring the wrong people for the role in the first place. Yet even more evidence suggests that sales professionals underperform because they are not inspired by their leader and are not being coached for success. By that I mean drilling deeper into developing the 'right' skills, traits and latent capabilities, and then aligning these with a malleable method.

High-performance sales professionals want to scale the tallest mountain. They also need to believe it's possible. Others demand to see what's possible—they need someone else to go there first. If it's not their fearless leader, a successful internal role model is critical in helping establish a new belief system and the confidence for what is ultimately attainable. Genuine high performers don't want to be managed. Who enjoys being managed, really? High performers come armed with an entrepreneurial mindset that sets them apart and gets things done. If you want to develop a high-performance sales culture, the term manager needs to be deleted from the vocabulary. In its place, use the more relevant title of leader.

Top salespeople are often promoted to manager, yet few are equipped with the sales leadership skills to lead and coach their team for success. A period of time away from the coalface actively selling can mean the methods they espouse are no longer relevant, particularly if the manager is too removed from the process and activity, or relies solely on feedback from team members. The feedback is nearly always biased. To counter this, the sales leader must be as actively involved in the sales process as possible. Successful leaders harness on-the-ground perspectives and communicate from a place of confidence and clarity. Strategy will only get you so far; high performance is driven more from action and experience. These two elements inspire respect and trust.

What salespeople are demanding, and essentially saying, in today's ever-changing and cautious markets is 'Lead me by example and show me what's possible. Then coach me for success! I want to download it, see it clearly and believe in it. Now that I'm clear, get out of the way and let me play with it!' Leading and coaching your sales team, as opposed to managing them, will help you to swiftly recognise and cut out genuine underperformers. It also inspires your team members to grow from a healthy culture that cultivates authentic leaders and teachers, instead of passengers.

> *Good leadership consists of showing average people*
> *how to do the work of superior people.*

John D. Rockefeller, American industrialist and philanthropist

Playful competition

You should always encourage competition in a team, but never let it compromise what your team stands for. Instead encourage team members to choose clients wisely and never compromise their values to get paid. Team competition is healthy when everyone is bound by mutual respect and is gently guided by clear and agreed terms of engagement.

Team competition becomes destructive when guidelines are ambiguous, rules are made on the fly and winning takes precedence over everything else. Your team won't have too much energy left to fight for your customers if they are too busy fighting each other, nor will they be focusing on creating valuable relationships if they are consumed by fulfilling their own agendas.

To create a successful team, a culture that rewards individual and team success is essential, but it should never be to the detriment of customers. Rewarding individual success on its own can de-motivate the less experienced team members and discourage them. Some managers promote this type of approach, but much like carrot and stick leadership—this is *old school* — thankfully we've evolved beyond it.

Is success measured in your team by:

- happy customers?

- creativity?

- innovation?

- profit?

- gross sales?

- annuity revenue?

- loyalty?

- entrepreneurialism?

- work ethic?

- passion?

The most common measurement of success is gross sales. This simple metric is rarely the best gauge of a successful team. These measurements are often misleading as most of the reality lies below surface. The most effective measure of a team's success is seen in two simple key metrics: one is work ethic and the other is their willingness to contribute to team members and customers. The most successful teams are competitive, sure, particularly when it comes to other companies in their space. They are fiercely competitive when it comes to getting the best out of themselves. Smart sales leaders reward team success above all else. If one person is clearly achieving more in a particular period, they encourage them to keep going, but also to help the others who aren't on par to succeed. This rewards their individual success, shares success intellectual property and, importantly, fosters a winning team culture. A team is only as successful as the weakest link. To drive your team forward you need to either remove the weak link altogether, and as a consequence make your collective smaller, or collectively work together to augment the weak link and make it stronger, and eventually unbreakable.

Rebel with a cause: Captain Paul Watson

Influencing with words and actions is far less challenging when you can see things from the other person's perspective. Empathy is magical and helps us connect with others, to feel and share their emotions. This is a true gift. Imagine living in a world without it? Along with empathy another quality sees those who are courageous enough to harness it become true masters of influence. I'm talking about fighting for a worthy cause—the true mark of an Outlaw. Many of history's greatest thought leaders and innovators have been Outlaws. They believed in their cause with such a passion and conviction that some of them even died fighting for it.

This fight is innate and lurks deep inside us all. To deny the fight is to deny the essence of the human spirit. Not to kill and harm, but to stand up, shout, defy ignorant rules and stand up for what you truly believe in. Only a minority of courageous people are prepared to fight and drive change but, to paraphrase the late, great pirate of

Silicon Valley, Steve Jobs, they are the ones who will make a dent in the universe.

Captain Paul Watson is a salty old sea dog making a monumental dent. The Canadian environmental activist is the founder of the Sea Shepherd Conservation Society. An awkward character, clearly outraged by ignorance, he is no stranger to the dark confines of a jail cell for living out his altruistic adventures. He and his crew dance with danger to traverse the Earth's dark and unforgiving oceans on a mission to prevent whale hunting. Sea Shepherd has been the most aggressive and successful whale-saving organisation in the world.

The captain's story began with a chance encounter with a wounded sperm whale. Staring into the whale's eye only moments from its death, he felt a deep pain, and this empathic experience has driven him to become one of the most passionate defenders of whales in history. Today, decades on, Watson is fighting as fiercely as ever to save these beautiful mammals. He puts the fear of god into the whalers he intercepts—endangering them and his own crew's lives as he barrels into their vessels and launches his ship in between the whale and the deadly harpoon. Read more of his inspiring story and the cause he has dedicated his life to fighting for at www. seashepherd.org.

In stark contrast to his early days, Watson now has some of the world's most influential people behind him—musicians, Hollywood actors and politicians—helping to promote his message and fund his mission to invest in the latest technology and marine resources. He is a testament to how, when your words and actions are purposefully aligned, and you are prepared to fight for what you believe in, this can be enough to drive change and it could just change the world.

I can assure you no whales are going to be killed today.

Captain Paul Watson, founder of the
Sea Shepherd Conservation Society

☞ Action points ✍

- Adapt your communication styles to align with your customers' preferences to fast-track engagement and begin to build trust.

- Map your Arc of Influence and determine who your decision maker, critical influencers, enablers and time-wasters are.

- Fight the fear: get off the email and pick up the Red Phone and activate your C Strategy!

CHAPTER 3

CREATE A CULT WITH PERSONALITY

You are most powerful, most effective when you are completely yourself.

Eckhart Tolle, author of *The Power of Now*

You and your competitors are all doing and selling the same thing in the same way. This makes it challenging for you to really stand out. It is, of course, possible to differentiate yourself with your preparation, the amount of time and energy you invest in each opportunity (dare to prepare), and by walking the talk, that is to say inspiring with your words and your actions. One area that requires less time, yet is still challenging to assert, is the concept of being true to yourself by simply being yourself. Identifying and developing your personal brand is essential for all sales professionals—especially how your personality connects with your target audience and gives them a true sense of commonality and mutual trust. To stand out in a cold, often crowded and competitive market, you have to be different, but if you keep playing the same game, you become mundane and your customers won't even see you—they will walk straight past. Moreover, if they do stop, you won't have a way of proving that you're different from everyone else, so the customer relationship defaults solely to price. Enter the price comparison gates at your own risk.

You may feel that who you are may well be boring compared with others—and that may be the reality for some people—but that's always relative. In any case you still need to bring more of yourself to what you do. You don't have to be overtly gregarious to be more appealing and personable to others: you can take a more personal approach to the way you do things or come up with new and interesting ways to present ideas and communicate your point of difference. Never dilute your personality in an attempt to be all things to all people, or you will be playing the same game. Show the world who you really are and what's truly important to you. Make your words dance with your actions, but also remember that, when you are true to yourself and you sell something you truly believe in, this level of confidence will not only influence your customers, it will illuminate a clear path for others. If you're not having fun being yourself and totally engrossed in what you're selling, I can guarantee your customers aren't enjoying the process either.

The secret selling ingredient

The most successful sales professionals are easily aroused by customers. They may appear normal at first glance, but if you peer a little closer there is something much more peculiar bubbling beneath the surface. These sales professionals aren't just fond of what they sell, they fantasise about it, removing themselves from the stresses of the everyday sales grind to a safe and warm place. They love what they sell and believe in it with an abnormal conviction.

The best salespeople in the world believe (rightly or wrongly) that their product or service is the best in their market. Each word that leaps from their lips is lubricated with so much confidence and sincerity the customer is helpless to deny it and is effortlessly seduced. You will come across these people in your travels. They can be found in almost all industries and parts of the world. Fearless, hungry, deeply passionate and driven, they will chew your ear off about what they sell. So certain, but always so convincing. Some people call these sales professionals evangelists. I simply call them nuts! But give me a team of nutty salespeople and I will show you a successful sales model. Nutty salespeople and value are a deadly mix.

The art of Chen

I arrived at Sydney airport. I briskly exited the terminal and was immediately greeted by the humid morning air. I waited for my ride in the line at the cab rank. After a few minutes, my cabby pulled up. The driver leaped out of his seat and charged around to my side of the car. A small Asian man bursting with energy greeted me. He snatched my suitcase, brushed past me and lobbed it into his boot. We both jumped in the cab.

He introduced himself, 'I'm Chen! Where are we off to today?' Slightly taken aback by Chen's lively demeanour, I responded, 'I'm presenting at a conference at the Novotel in Manly.' Apparently stunned by this, Chen burst into a cheer, 'Manly. Okay, this is my lucky day!'

We headed through Sydney's Domain tunnel. The traffic was backed up. Sensing my anxiety about being late for a speaking gig seemed to infuriate Chen—he profusely apologised for the delay and assured me that I would not be late for my 11 am start. Though slightly perplexed by Chen's concern for my professional wellbeing, I got the impression he genuinely cared about getting me to my destination on time. As we cruised through Neutral Bay, we shared a joke and Chen asked about my business and the nature of my presentation. He then asked if I had kids, and if my travels took me away from my family often. I said it did sometimes. With pursed lips he glared sideways at me, and in a ponderous tone, explained that he was genuinely concerned for me and that family was the most important thing in life. I couldn't help but be intrigued by this man and his strange ways.

Chen put his foot down when he needed to, to my amusement and distress, and got me to the venue with plenty of time to spare. Chen hit the skids and the embattled cab's brakes squealed in pain as we came to an abrupt stop. With one foot on the brake and his head cocked towards me, Chen blurted out in a proud tone, 'We are here boss, on time! Are you happy?'

'Chen, you're a legend. Thank you and I would like to give you a tip.'

'No, no, boss, not needed. What time will I pick you up?'

'Oh, back to the airport? Okay, well not tomorrow, but the following day at 12.30 pm?'

Chen ripped a business card out of his wallet and declared, 'I'll be here at 12 just in case you early, and if you late, I wait. Okay?'

You can guess my response.

Two days later, I finished my speaking engagement. I was then caught up chatting with some of the participants. Consumed by the conference and still running on adrenaline I had completely forgotten about my commitment to meet Chen. It was now just after 1 pm. I exited the foyer, suitcase in tow and scanned the hotel entrance for a taxi. To my delight, my eyes quickly landed on a small man who was bursting with energy. I was 30 minutes late but that mattered little to my new mate Chen.

I don't know about you, but getting a taxi ride can be either a dreary or a downright stinky experience. We have all sat in the passenger seat gagging for air as our ears bleed to the sounds of loud music. With Chen, the trip seemed to pass in much less time. Despite his cab looking shabby and like it was being eaten alive by rust, I didn't mind taking the journey with him: in fact, that added to the experience, which was far from ordinary.

Chen had created an experience for me that was unique and memorable. Amazingly, it cost him nothing but a positive tone, and a genuine interest in me and my best interests. Chen defies the rules and drives change by not buying in to the poor industry standards set by other taxi drivers. You don't have to be Nostradamus to know who I will be calling when I next need a cab ride in Sydney—my man, Chen! Because he's that good and he makes me feel that special. Forget the bells and whistles and slick marketing messages: Chen delivers something much more important, and in return I give him my business and loyalty.

Your silent sales weapon

The difference between one person smashing their annual target or just making their budget, or becoming a world-class influencer, can be measured by the quality of the conversations they are having with the right people. Equally vital, and one of the most critical human features, is our willingness and ability to listen and tailor our communication specifically to the other person. Being interesting also matters, and one of the best ways you can be more interesting to others is to demonstrate a genuine interest in them. This can be augmented by delivering more meaningful and purposeful questions, based on the information you are receiving.

We have all met someone who is a poor listener, and we often judge them as being either ignorant or arrogant. We then make an assessment of their personality based on that. However, when you're selling, this is the salesperson's problem, not the customer's. Just because a customer doesn't listen intently to you doesn't mean they're not interested in you: it could mean they absorb information in a different manner from you. Being conscious of these differences can help you dramatically enhance your ability to connect with and influence people.

Three styles of learning

Human beings learn through three key styles:

- *Auditory*—these people prefer to learn through listening; for example, to the radio or to someone speaking in a conversation or lecture.

- *Visual*—these people prefer to learn by seeing things mapped out in pictures, diagrams or the written word.

- *Kinaesthetic*—these people prefer to learn through touching and feeling; they may prefer to play with things or take them apart to learn.

The first step in understanding how to more effectively engage with others is to know your own natural learning style and how you prefer to consume information. Knowing how you absorb information is important because it also provides you with an insight into how others absorb the same information. Employ a combination of communication styles to encapsulate all three learning preferences. And incorporate methods for learning about your clients before meeting them and during meetings, so you can adapt your style and the content delivery to focus more on their learning preference.

To find out about your customer's learning style you need to ask them questions and then really listen to their responses and gauge their reactions. Remember that 55 per cent of their response will be in their body language, 35 per cent though the tonality of their voice and their expression, and only 10 per cent in words. This can make what they say very different from what they actually mean. Their body language and tone will help you understand what they are really saying. For example, if, halfway through your pitch (auditory preference), you see your customer's eyes glazing over, this is the chance to change your approach, so stop the conversation and move over to a whiteboard or pull out a writing pad and start mapping out your ideas (visual preference), so they can see them. If that lacks impact, then offer them an opportunity to play with your ideas by getting them involved more to enhance their input (kinaesthetic preference). What and how you do this is up to you, just don't make the mistake of applying one communication technique to varying learning preferences. Words are meaningless without emotion, and your relationships won't be very meaningful until you start really listening. And it's often the space between the words that provides the real meaning behind what is being said.

A soft skill that's hard to master

Listening skills are an essential ingredient in any person's success. Listening is a soft skill that is hard to master. Often when a person believes they are listening to another person, they are actually listening to the sound of their own internal dialogue, and waiting for an opportunity to speak next.

Listening is a learned skill. It takes work. Most people default to non-listening and open listening. In these engagement states the words are the focus. The person may appear to be listening, but they are just hearing and responding to the words that are being spoken.

As we know, words count for only a small part of how we influence people. Most influential is our body language, followed by our tonality. When you understand this and also look for the silent undercurrent, that is to say the emotions behind the words, you start to get a clearer sense of what is really being said. You start to really listen and connect.

Active listening skills and awareness for guiding the conversation and asking probing and clarifying questions ensure you're actively engaged in the conversation.

The skill of heart listening takes active listening to a higher level, where you are not only hearing and guiding the conversation, but also applying total focus to the other person, which allows you to gain awareness of their energy, emotions and attitudes. You also tap into the underlying tone or impact of the conversation, and where it is taking you and the other person. You're looking for and connecting with their emotions.

Heart listening allows you to more accurately assess and gently guide the conversation and genuinely connect with the other person. It is at this depth of listening that your intuition will be most available to you and will provide you with the most information possible about the heart of the issue for your customer, and their underlying goals and aspirations.

Once you have identified the emotions that your customer is feeling, acknowledging those emotions demonstrates to the customer that you have empathy for them, and since the buying process is driven largely by emotions, acknowledging these emotions is the key!

Slowing things down where possible, going deeper and really being present in each conversation is not only a more pleasurable and thoughtful way to engage people, it also demonstrates something much more powerful: that you care about how the other person feels. This is an essential part in being a person of influence and a truly masterful salesperson.

Listen to many, speak to a few.

William Shakespeare, playwright

Tips to harness the skill of heart listening

- Slow things down—breathe and be conscious of your own energy state first.

- Always make eye contact—don't just stare, but be aware and truly connect.

- Pause before responding—don't cut the other person off in the middle or before the end of their sentence.

- Resist the temptation to habitually divert the conversation back to you and your story.

- Probe and ask clarifying questions to draw out their higher goals and aspirations.

- Drill deeper with masterful questions that engage the other person on a deeper level.

- Align their body language and tonality to what is being said.

- Paraphrase and emphasise the emotions they are conveying to you.

- Connect the emotions to their higher goals and aspirations.

A modern-day Robin Hood: Richard Branson

How does a dyslexic high-school dropout become a multi-billionaire? Today, people fly in his aeroplanes, shop at his stores, attend his sold-out public speaking events, and will soon soar into the heavens in his spaceships. Richard Branson defies the rules not only in business but also in life. He picks fights with the big boys: his mission is to take on corporate Goliaths that aren't serving their customers to the required standard and providing their customers with a Virgin alternative. He is a man determined to fight for what he believes in and have fun while doing it.

Branson's wispy grey locks and Cheshire cat grin are never far from a publicity stunt. He uses almost all aspects of his life to promote the Virgin brand, from his outrageous record-breaking attempts in hot-air balloons and Atlantic crossings, to his family getaway on Necker Island that Branson also uses to host gatherings such as The Elders, a collection of wise and influential people that work towards addressing global social issues. His life is carefully recorded on a canvas like an oil painting that we can all admire from afar. Branson comes across as your average Joe — everyone's favourite uncle. But underneath his unassuming, almost nonchalant facade, is a man fiercely driven to defy the rules and make a difference. A modern-day Robin Hood who robs the rich and distributes to the poor, he fights to give his customers more.

Richard Branson was in a marketing session with the key marketing executives and staff at Virgin. The marketers were labouring over the exact message they wanted the brand to convey, with various opinions taking the conversation in different directions. After long, heated discussion, which had resulted in no clear agreement, Richard, who had spent most of the time listening, strolled to the front of the room. He approach a whiteboard riddled with scribble and pithy strap lines. He feverishly erased all the jargon. He then slowly scribed two large words onto the whiteboard in scratchy letters:

ROBIN HOOD

Nodding his head knowingly, he then faced the team of marketing gurus and scoffed, 'That's it ... that's who we are: Robin Hood.' He then walked out.

There may be an element of myth to that story, but don't be like the team of marketing executives and get too caught up in the jargon, and don't over-think your value proposition. When you commit to a business and ethos that is both simple and meaningful to your customers, invariably what follows are not only customers, but also loyal advocates who will promote your personal brand.

Own your mistakes or they will own you

I was three hours late after my flight was delayed due to fog and inclement weather. In a panicked state, I rushed to pick up my hire car while apologising over the phone to my client and assuring her I wasn't far away, and started on the 60-minute trek to my new business pitch. Driving with a sense of defeat, I questioned whether my many hours of preparation, the flight and now my pained efforts would be all in vain. Being late to a key presentation seldom sets a positive tone, and negative first impressions are always challenging to overcome. My sat-nav directed me safely through fog and lashing rain to my destination. I pulled up, checked in with reception and after a swift set-up, launched into my presentation.

It's easy to blame factors beyond your control for letting people down. In this instance, I could have confidently blamed the airline, but I didn't. (The airline failed to offer even a token gesture for inconveniencing their passengers — in particular those who delayed others or missed meetings altogether, and some who no doubt lost money or goodwill as a result.) In my introduction, I not only apologised to the 10 stakeholders who had rearranged their schedules to meet me — I also offered a gesture of goodwill to demonstrate my regret. They all accepted and appeared comfortable with my barter. This gesture did cost me (as I will explain later), but the price is insignificant if it puts customers at ease and helps to win back their trust. It is one thing to make an apology, quite another to do something about it. If you let a client down, even when circumstances are out of your control, do your best to demonstrate your disappointment. Offer a discount, something low cost but of high perceived value, or something small yet meaningful. Often a sorry just won't cut it, so make your apology real and tangible. This helps to rebuild goodwill and you may just turn your negative into a positive. Correcting an error in a thoughtful way can, and usually does, galvanise your relationship and make it even stronger. A few days later, this client gave me the go ahead—this award-winning credit union, Community Alliance, is now one of my favourite clients.

I honoured the promise to demonstrate my regret for being late for the initial pitch. Mid afternoon on the final day of the training program, six Harley-Davidson motorcycles rumbled into the car park and all the stakeholders were taken on a wild ride. Not only was the experience exhilarating, it also reinforced a key element of the program of brand values. But most of all it proved a point. If you build a reputation as being someone who is genuinely interested in helping others and a person who keeps their word, even if it costs them, this is a part of your personality that no-one can ever question.

It's big to be small

We naturally sell to and buy from people we like or share a likeness with. How many of your customers fly to work in their own chartered jet? You don't have to be big to compete in today's markets—quite the contrary in fact. The game has changed: big teams have been reduced and replaced by the internet. Big offices have been traded for hot-desking and home offices. And there are multimillion-dollar lounge-room operations playing with the big boys every day—and often winning!

What does being small signify? It means being agile, flexible, responding in real time and fast off the mark! It also means being adaptive and responsive to change, or, even better, being the company driving change! The bigger you are the less nimble and able to adapt to quick shifts and changes in the market you will be. Things change fast in today's economy, and if you don't respond and adapt, you could very soon be out of the game. The smaller and leaner you are, the more energy you store. Big, heaving companies burn masses of energy just to keep the doors open. They are lethargic and lack energy. If you think you're working for or leading a company like that, hit the scales now and modify your appetite and what you think you need to eat to succeed.

I spend a significant portion of my own time helping big sales teams focus their time and energy on increasing their output. In many cases, that provides them with tools to do more with less: to help them think small and focus on small tasks, then to do them over and over again, until they are exceptional at what they do. To attract and retain top talent your business will need to create an inspiring environment for likeminded salespeople to do their thing. Bigger is rarely better in this instance, particularly when it comes to growing your sales force. Give me the 20 per cent of high-performers, over the 80 per cent who are just making up the numbers any day. If you can't be small, then at least start to think small. Start by making your smallest stakeholders—your customers—big.

I began a revolution with 82 men. If I had to do it again, I'd do it with 10 or 15 and absolute faith. It does not matter how small you are if you have faith and a plan of action.

Fidel Castro, Cuban revolutionary leader

Your time to thrive

Cast your mind back to 65 million years ago. It's a mild afternoon. Striking pink and orange shades of light paint the horizon. Forests and jungles are lush. The air is pure. Seas are hundreds of metres higher than today. The Earth is a sphere of splendour and energy. Giant beasts roam and dominate the Earth. Salivating meat-eating predators, along with their long-necked tree-foraging relatives, panic the ground-dwellers. Mighty birds the size of a bus glide through the air with wings that cast a vast dark shadow onto the ground below. This is a terrifying time to be a small, earth-bound creature.

Our world, like the world in the age of the dinosaurs, is overshadowed by large ignorant beasts. Corrupt power brokers are largely to blame for the world's current economic turmoil. Another cataclysmic blast, like the one that brought the end of the dinosaurs and like the GFC of recent times, will occur within the next decade caused by debt-addicted institutions and governments. We are already seeing the US and parts of Europe being battered by financial meteors. The average punter that believes their destiny is determined by higher powers will be in for a rude awakening.

To attach your long-term wellbeing and financial security to a dinosaur is a losing strategy. I pick up a newspaper and all I read is pain and suffering. I turn on the six o'clock news only to consume more fear and struggle. If I believed the hype, I might as well fall on my sword where I stand. The lesson is don't trust a dinosaur and pay scant regard to the media. Despite what's going on around you, take it upon yourself to carve your own path. Drive change and focus on your strengths. You are small, nimble and able to seek refuge quickly. Keep your eyes peeled, your head up and your cost-base low, and partner with other small creatures to amplify your capabilities and play big.

I'm most inspired by the little guys, the likes of the shop merchants, the artists, the restaurateurs and the consultants who are bursting with their own authentic personality. People who don't want to grow too big: for them, it's not about awards and being the fastest growing franchise — it's about the experience. It's about delivering more value and contributing by providing customers with something meaningful. It's about being the best you can be and doing what you love. It's being true to yourself and not conforming to others. It's being true to you and your customers connecting with this and coming back time and again, and bringing their friends. That's inspiring to me.

Dinosaurs were huge, clumsy beasts with small brains. You, on the other hand are smart and agile. The business you are working for may be a corporate monster, but you can still think small and harness an entrepreneurial spirit. Take action and be accountable. Be known as a person of integrity and someone who gets the job done right. Take these trying times as an opportunity to see our world differently—as an opportunity for victory! It's your time to thrive.

> *Be faithful in small things because*
> *it is in them that your strength lies.*
>
> Mother Teresa of Calcutta

Be the cause not the effect

As salespeople, if we had a choice we would prefer to deal only with customers we liked, that is, those whose personalities we most connect with. People similar to us. Yet this is rarely the case. As we established in the previous chapter on social styles, when we sell we will come across four predominant communication styles: thinker, director, socialiser and relater. When you understand the differences in styles you can work to minimise the differences and build stronger connections. That being said, we may still meet people who are difficult to manage or get along with. Do you have to like your customers? Of course not, but in my experience, the better you relate to and connect with your customers, the more meaningful and durable your relationship becomes. The more willing the customer will be to open up and provide you with information to help you tailor your approach and really hit the mark with your solution. You don't like your customers, but you must at the very least share a likeness with them. The best form of likeness is always taking an interest in their best interests.

'I don't really like you, but I still really care about you.' This is a powerful mantra I embed into every customer service–oriented businesses. Even if you don't like the personality of some of your customers, you should still better-service the pants off them, and enjoy doing it. Is that idealistic? Yes, of course it is, but in today's hyper-competitive environment, anything less is settling for mediocrity and we all know how that story ends.

Without commonality all human relationships become surface level— 'take 'em or leave 'em', and 'easy come, easy go'—you know how it goes. Relationships like this offer little intrinsic or lasting value to either party, making them transactional. I am still staggered by the number of companies that take an easy come, easy go approach to customer relationship development. It's as if they believe there is a never-ending supply of happy customers lined up with their eyes shut and wallets open. I'm also not surprised by these companies having limited success.

I make a living by helping sales- and service-driven companies find the most value and performance from their sales activities and customer relationships, so in my world, sales and service go hand in hand. Yet so many companies fail to understand this. They try hard to win new business, and often do, yet they still allow someone along the value chain to let the customer down, in a small or significant way, leaving the self-respecting customer with little choice but to move on. In the process taking their valuable repeat business and friends with them.

The best way of fulfilling your own interest is to take care of others.

Dalai Lama, Tibetan Buddhist spiritual leader

Three little words to radically boost your retail sales

If you're operating a retail company and not driving a social strategy, you are missing the mark. But the retail industry, by and large, has more serious issues to contend with. The traditional retail industry worldwide is in meltdown. Sales are declining, while the online retail space is growing rapidly, and for good reason. Not only is shopping on the internet speedy and convenient, we also don't have to suffer torturous exchanges with frontline staff who are simply not there or couldn't care less about us when they do show up. Let's resist the urge to solely blame the internet for the decline in retail sales: it's certainly an important factor, but so is the blatant lack of duty of care from retail staff. Think about this: what self-respecting customer would willingly frequent a retail environment that made them feel unimportant, or worse, like a burden? Many of us have experienced standing at a counter for an extended period anxiously waiting, waiting… only to be met by a salesperson who acts as if they are doing us a favour by serving us.

Retailers take note: every customer that enters your retail environment has three words emblazoned on their forehead: 'I am important'. Why, you ask? Because they are not only paying for the product, they are paying for the experience — the customer experience.

Showing more personality can be as simple as remembering these three little words. Fail to recall them and you may as well shut up shop and put a big neon sign on the front door that reads, 'Gone online!' Customers are prepared to embrace the adage, 'If you want something done right, do it yourself'. *Click!*

Only a few years ago Australian banks did a commendable job driving change and successfully pushing their customers to self-service online and by reducing the number of their branches and tellers, forcing customers to endure long lines and waits if they persisted in using bank branches. This was a cost-saving exercise carefully disguised as customer convenience. Collectively they soon learned this approach eroded their customer loyalty. Now the banks are scrambling to herd customers back to the branch and retail environments in order to cross-sell and upsell products, having learned just how critical personal interactions are for the success of any brand. Apple gets it. Customers camp overnight outside a new Apple experience store to buy the latest products. Madness really! Or is there more to it? We all search for positive and meaningful experiences every day. One of the best ways to help your customers find a meaning is through good old-fashioned service. We all crave it. It's not expensive to deliver either. In fact it's the most cost-effective strategy that I know of to build brand loyalty.

The internet is an awesome tool, so harness it. But also make sure every touch point promotes your product or service and brand in a compelling and relevant way, and yes this includes sale and service people above all. Be sure to educate, invest in and train your retail sales team on the nuances of meaningful customer service. Yes, some of them will move on, but keep training and developing them. If your business is really about customer service, you need to back that up with hard evidence. The best evidence can be seen very quickly in the quality of your people. At the very least make sure they understand the three little words that matter most to every single customer: I am important.

A flower a day keeps dull service away

I stood three deep in a queue that seemed to be moving backwards compared with the other aisles. At the head of the line was an elderly woman laughing and chatting with the checkout chick. They appeared to be having a gay old time. But I was decomposing in my own anxiety, hot and noticeably bothered. Just let me pay for my stuff and get out of here!

The lady eventually paid for her groceries. She waved goodbye and then gleefully snatched her bags and wandered off. Finally we were moving. I quickly twitched my toes to make sure they were still there. With nowhere else to look, I slowly looked up — oh great, the checkout chick was now chewing the ears off the 40-something man just ahead of me. Chatting and giggling, never losing eye contact while she nodded with an empathetic rhythm and leisurely scanned his groceries. What is this, happy hour? I pursed my lips and shook my head in distress. Their conversation dragged on, until the man paid and then scooted off with a smile.

Finally, I was next, and it's about bloody time, I thought. 'Hi there, how's your day going?' blurted the checkout chick. 'Fine thanks.' I responded with a sigh. In a bubbly tone she then asked what I was doing on such a sunny Sunday. I told her I was on a business trip. She probed deeper and I proceeded to respond to all her questions. All the while I couldn't help but gawk at the three small yellow flowers she had carefully intertwined into the side of her auburn locks. Before I knew it, I was immersed in a conversation. My agitation, caused by the summer heat and a long queue, had vaporised.

I was so entertained by the flower lady's demeanour and interest in me that I didn't see her swipe my groceries, but they magically appeared in my shopping bag. I had paid and now it was time to move on. With a smile now stretched across my face I thanked the flower lady, said goodbye and skipped out of the grocery store.

Truly exceptional customer service is one of the best ways to promote your brand's personality. Like preparation, it's almost impossible to overdo: I dare you to over-prepare. I also dare you to over-service your customers. The default setting akin to preparation is to under-service. Game-changing customer service, truly impactful and meaningful service, can be very hard to find, but when you find it, you will know about it! So much so you'll be inspired to tell others about your experience. When someone goes out of their way to recognise us and help us, it lights us up. All it takes is a keen ear and intent to learn about people and acknowledge who they really are. This is so simple to do that it's often overlooked. To blossom in a competitive market, take a leaf from the flower lady. You won't just illuminate your customer's day—you will light up your own too. And your customers will be transformed from mere transactions to cult-like followers.

The best way to find yourself is to lose yourself in the service of others.

Mahatma Gandhi, father of the Indian
independence movement

Friends with benefits

One of the most valuable assets you can create in business is what I call a friendship with benefits. Not the touchy-feely kind: rather an enduring relationship between a customer and the vendor that contributes to both in a valuable and meaningful way. Acquaintances, we can take or leave. Typically surface level, these relationships hold little lasting value. Unfortunately, most customers are treated this way, because the staff are not usually empowered with the right knowledge and skills to do better.

How you treat people in a commercial situation shouldn't differ that much from a social setting. The same non-negotiable essentials must always apply, such as empathy, common courtesy, respect, keeping our promises, saying what we mean, being true to ourselves, and above all showing a genuine interest in the other party's best interests. Think about the people we consider friends. What behaviours do they demonstrate towards us? How do we treat them? How long have we known them? Why are they so important to us? What really attracts us to them? Do we genuinely trust them with our secrets? More than anything else, we are attracted to friends because of how they make us feel.

We can share a laugh or divulge our innermost fears and insecurities. We spend time getting to know who they really are and what's really important to them. We probe and drill deeper to the heart of what they mean or are trying to tell us, even if the conversation is prickly or awkward. Friends don't try to blatantly profit from us, without, of course, being swiftly removed from our social group. Friends, more often than not, are highly adept at listening to us—and your best friend is exceptional at that.

As a customer, I prefer to buy from someone I like and trust. I hate being sold something: instead, I want to be empowered with information. Critical information solves my problems or opens up my eyes and helps me shed light on an area that will radically transform what I do or what I'm setting out to achieve. I detest being smothered by self-focused communication and marketing jargon. I crave to be heard and understood. I want to be empowered. And if there's a problem, I need to know that you, the salesperson, my trusted adviser, are there for me.

It is said that you can measure a person by the quality of their friends. This is true. The principle applies profoundly to businesses too. Ironically, being a true friend isn't all that hard, but it does take effort. And customers aren't really that complex to understand—you should know, because you're one too. Good friends are hard to find, so never be a salesperson: always be a friend with benefits and let your personality shine through.

RetroService activity

Here's an activity to help you and your team members bring more personality to your customers with meaningful service. Gather up your customer-facing team members, as many as you like, and break them into small teams. Nominate a leader for each team. Break out the marker pens and butcher's paper. You don't need an easel, simply pin the paper to a nearby wall. Now you're ready for some RetroService action. Each team leader leads the discussion and facilitates drawing out the relevant insights for their team. Brainstorm and then list on your paper as many ways you can think of that would bring back old-fashioned service to your organisation. Benchmark industry leaders or companies in related industries that demonstrate outstanding customer service. Think of a time or place where you received exceptional customer service. How did it make you feel and what were you compelled to do? Discuss this with the group and then mark it all down. Once complete, make a short list and then assign people to actions, outcomes and time frames. Giddy up!

☞ Action points ☜

- You need to stand out from the crowd and be more interesting than your competitors. Be more interested to be more interesting.

- Harness your secret weapons: your ears. Listen for the silent undercurrent and get to the heart of what is truly being said. Develop more meaningful relationships by genuinely caring and listening.

- Bring back old-fashioned service: RetroService.

- Don't forget the three little words that make a big impact: *I am important.*

- Keep your communication simple and focused on the benefits for your customers. Think Robin Hood.

CHAPTER 4

HARNESS THE POWER OF PROCESS

*The unlike is joined together, and from differences
results the most beautiful harmony.*

Heraclitus, ancient Greek philosopher

Process is essential in all areas of business. Process creates
efficiencies. Some industries are inherently more process-
driven than others. When we think of process our minds
usually draw a picture of a manufacturing plant. We don't
often see an artist or a creative person in this scenario. Yet
even the most artistic people work to a form of process to
manifest their inspiration.

Process is the mother of replication

In sales, a successful process allows you to work by a
consistent set of operating principles that guide and support
you and the customer towards realising a predetermined
outcome. This outcome can then be replicated time and
again, and if the process is handed to another, they too can
realise the same outcome using the same method. A lack of

expertise in moving customers through the right sales process is commonly flagged by management as a lack of effort or skills among their salespeople. More accurately, both these points of failure are symptoms of a much larger problem: poor process. In this instance, where the process starts or finishes is usually determined by customers, not salespeople, leaving the salesperson disempowered.

A doctor follows a carefully tested method for identifying and determining a patient's appropriate course of medical treatment. A builder has a process for moving a project from plan to lock-up stage. Similarly, athletes adhere to processes to maximise their performance. Equally, all salespeople are more efficient and successful when they work according to a simple and well-defined process. Process can be as simple as three steps or as complex and elaborate as you require. In my experience, processes are most potent when they are simple to understand, execute and measure. Each step of a process should provide both the salesperson and customer with the right information to make the right decision in order to ratchet the process forward.

Your best salespeople are probably already working by a conscious or unconscious sales process. If the process is really working and getting results, the process needs to be identified, defined and mapped, and then followed by all team members. Regular training, collaborative strategy sessions and role-playing help to embed a sales process into a team and ensure that it is consistently utilised and adhered to. The key word here is buy-in. If salespeople don't understand the benefits of the process or don't trust it, they won't engage with it.

A strong process will also lend itself to being measured. This makes measuring team members more effective as you can work out their areas for development and model their strengths and capability areas for development. The beauty of a successful sales process is that even less experienced salespeople can make it work. Be mindful, however, that the right process in the wrong hands can cause untold destruction. Such is the power of process.

Simplicity is the ultimate sophistication.

Leonardo da Vinci, Renaissance artist

Mad Max: value your time or no-one else will

I recall driving, for the fourth time in two weeks, to a potential client's office for a meeting, the trek taking me just over an hour from my office. On that day, I walked into the business with my eyes open and a wide smile. I was greeted by the friendly receptionist with a youthful glow, who said with a puzzled look, 'Hi, Trent, what are you doing here?' With a neck twitch, I responded, 'I'm here to see Max.'

'Hmm, that's odd, we have already hired a new web company.' She then nervously giggled, 'Anyway, I'll just get Max for you.'

I could feel the air being sucked out of the reception area. My blood slowly began to simmer under my suit. I walked into Max's office and could immediately sense he was not himself. After a bit of small talk, I proceeded as planned, concealing my knowledge of the exchange with the receptionist.

'So, Max, I've got the revised paperwork here. Given we have already discussed this several times, let's just get down to business shall we? If you could just read these amended items and confirm these revised sections with your initials, all I need is your signature here, and we can commence the project as soon as next week.'

Max squirmed in his seat. 'Oh, about that. I need some more time. My partner is away this week and I'll need him to okay this.'

I said nothing, but my glare swarmed with insolence. My lack of response was excruciating for both of us. So Max continued to fill the void of silence between us with more untruths.

'All should be okay mate, just leave it with me and I'll fax it through next week.'

In search of the truth I proceeded to push forward, knowing Max didn't know I knew he had already signed with someone else. 'That's okay, Max. Look, just sign here and if you need to change your mind for any reason just give me a call and we can amend accordingly.' I again pushed the contract towards him and picked up my pen and slowly placed it next to the sign here section. His anxiety was palpable.

With nowhere to flee, Max switched to fight mode. Agitated, he stood up and charged towards the door. In a belligerent tone, be blurted out, 'Look, I'm not signing anything today, like I said, I'll speak with my partner and I may be in contact next week.'

'May?' I thought to myself.

'Now if you don't mind, I've got to get to another meeting and I am starting to lose my patience.'

'Max, please sit down! I'm not going anywhere until you please explain to me what is really going on. I know you have hired another company, so why on earth did you agree to this meeting and have me drive over an hour here to see you again?'

His eyes glazed over as he mumbled and fumbled around for some inadequate words of condolence, 'Look, you're a nice bloke. I didn't have the heart to tell you, given all the effort and time you've put in. My business partner made the call last week and it was out of my control, sorry.' And with that, I huffed and puffed, and blew his house down.

Not quite: I scrambled out with my tail in one hand and an unsigned proposal in the other.

This was an unpleasant experience, but to add insult to injury, this was not an isolated incident: many of my team members were suffering similar frustrations. In the early stages of this particular business, my team and I spent most of our time chasing new business opportunities: pushing and driving, identifying perceived problems and then ramming our solutions home with clever and calculated negotiation tactics. However, the business was losing money and going backwards. In short, my salespeople were all as desperate as I was. And most of the time we were ignoring our intuition to chase time-wasters.

To overcome and safeguard against time-wasting prospects who would gladly take our time and information with no intention of ever buying from us, we introduced more substance and structure by mapping our sales process step by step and training all team members to follow it meticulously, while also adding their own personality and flavour to it where needed. We also began charging a small fee for our pre-sales work, which included creative concepts and proposals. This allowed the team to invest more time and resources into the proposal, which increased the value for the customers. It also required time and insights from the client, which enhanced their level of buy-in. This was something no-one else in the industry was doing at the time, so it created a point of difference, but most importantly it began attacking time waste immediately. This approach seemed radical at the time, but it was necessary, although it met with resistance from some team members and customers. However, by and large, as we grew in confidence in selling the process and communicating its benefits to the right customers, our method of working by and trusting our process helped to transform our little company from just a handful of staff to one of the industry's largest in only a few short years.

Collaborate to innovate

The collaborative process is a powerful way to engage team members and customers, but it also provides a platform to merge skills and game-changing ideas. When it comes to summoning the creative forces, man is not an island. Our world is full of people who can contribute enormous value in their own way, yet most are never seen or heard. As a society, we seldom encourage others to take a path of risk and unbridled adventure because this approach is untested and has the potential to break conventions and reputations. Who is going to pay for true innovation anyway, your employer or your customers? Hmm—good luck with that. Most of us are trained to do things based on what someone else has already done, and that's okay, but being led to believe it's the best and only way isn't okay. To drive change you will need to abandon certainty and venture into the dark unknown realms of possibility.

Next time you're in a team meeting and a colleague offers an ambitious idea, before you shoot them down in flames or passively disengage, take a moment to offer some constructive thinking around their suggestion. I encourage you to encourage a team culture that supports, not only each other, but also the development of bold and ambitious goals. You don't need to have your head in the clouds all the time, but being on the ground all day doesn't serve you either. You need to have a balance of pragmatism and a willingness to see things from a higher perspective. This is one of the most effective ways to rise above what is and see the path that leads to what can be. What holds many people back in life isn't lack of skills; it's their unwillingness to share more of themselves with others. They fear being rejected, particularly if what they believe in is against the commonly held beliefs of their tribe. They believe they are not good enough and fear being judged and rejected as a consequence. So, it's up to you to inspire them to see more, feel more and be more in life. Why is it up to you? You're a leader and that's what leaders do.

Tips to inspire innovation in your team

- Declare innovation as part of your culture and elect champions to lead it.
- Set up a taskforce responsible for implementing grand ideas and bold ideals.
- Support and encourage innovation through recognition.
- If you're passionate about a great idea, fight for it!
- Launch one great idea or bold ideal per financial quarter.
- Reward people not only for results, but also for engagement and participation.
- Get everyone involved—inspiration can come from anywhere and anyone.
- When a great idea bombs, be accountable, and learn and grow from it.
- When a great idea flies and really takes off, celebrate and share the success with everyone.

Collaboration in action—99designs

99designs is the largest online marketplace for crowd-sourced graphic design services, and it enables businesses to source a range of creative outputs such as logo design, web-page design, print design and other graphic design work quickly and affordably. The business promotes design projects to a global community of nearly 150 000 designers in more than 190 countries. Having recently used 99designs, I have to say the model is brilliant. For our logo design we received more than 170 design variations. We had no obligation to select and pay for a winner, but we did. Our total investment was just under $500. I recall paying a designer, just one year ago, $750 for three variations of a single design. I'm now a big 99designs fan, such is the power of the collaborative process.

> *In the long history of humankind ... those who learned to collaborate and improvise most effectively have prevailed.*
>
> Charles Darwin, author of *The Origin of Species*

More crazy customers

In my previous book, *The Naked Salesman*, I explored the damaging effects that crazy customers, or time-wasters, have on businesses by eating your precious time and diverting your attention away from genuine and valuable customers. Crazy customers can manifest from pushy salespeople who are too persuasive for their own good. Crazy customers can also be created by the right salespeople using the wrong process, or the wrong salespeople using the right process. Like Mad Max, crazy customers are also those who are seeking free information for their own, often deceptive, purposes. There are crazies everywhere.

Inexperienced salespeople will impetuously start pounding the cash register as soon as someone calls them, believing that when a potential customer initiates the contact, they are a hot prospect and their intentions must be genuine. This is not always the case. In fact, there are perils in this belief. In a perfect (of course impossible) world, we would all much rather spend our time pursuing flaming hot in-bound enquiries than sniffing around and hunting them out.

The internet has been the greatest incubator of crazy customers the world has ever seen. Anyone, whether genuine, ambivalent or even deceptive, can do a quick search on Google or bust open an app and then blast an enquiry—not just to you, but also to most of your competitors. And this is achieved in only a few short minutes. Treat all web enquiries with a filtering process and manoeuvre them accordingly. Not all enquiries are created equal: this is where your process comes in.

By developing an effective qualification process that doesn't alienate potential legitimate customers, you give yourself more chance of identifying the crazies early, which saves you time, resources and money. Understanding your existing clients will help you work out a new client's relevance and importance to your business, so when someone contacts you, you are already armed with insights that will enable you to profile them and give you confidence that you are talking with the right person to then begin your sales conversation.

The insights that come from an analysis of your existing customer base are also critical for outbound lead generation activities, such as the Red Phone (see chapter 2), as they provide your team with greater clarity and confidence to target more effectively, eliminating crazies expediently along the way.

Indecent proposal

Randy is an IT consultant. Every week enthusiastic potential customers seek him out with a range of problems he can solve and of course the money to help him solve them. Today's meeting is no different, and at the end they shake hands. Randy leaves with a fervent, 'I'll start our process and get a proposal to you by the end of the week!' He struts back to his cubicle and nonchalantly invests his employer's precious resources into another opportunity.

He fills his sales pipe and adds the details to the whiteboard. The potential gross sales figure is then inserted into his spreadsheet. Life is good.

However, there's a catch: this is the twentieth proposal Randy has written in the last three months and not one of them has been dropped. Moreover, Randy has spent so much time chasing these irresistible opportunities he has neglected his own outbound sales and marketing activities. His sales pipe projects almost a six zero figure, but the real figure is closer to zero. Randy is now forced to chase hard, but he soon realises there's a common theme beginning to emerge: no-one is returning his calls. The sales manager starts to apply the blowtorch. Now Randy can't seem to get a break, and so he decides this isn't the right company for him and resigns. His ego is intact but his credibility has cracked.

Randy's story is a common one, especially for those who rely solely on inbound enquiries for their success. All of Randy's opportunities were being facilitated by the client—in other words, the client determined the process. Although this approach seems easier than outbound marketing, in reality Randy had no way of replicating success even if he had stumbled upon it, because he hadn't developed a successful process. For a smarter approach, he needed a balance of proven outbound relationship development activities and methods for manoeuvring inbound enquiries. Akin to my experience with Mad Max, Randy could have charged a fee for his consultation at the front end of the sales process to filter out time-wasters, or chunked his process down to ensure each step established the required buy-in and reduced the risk for all parties.

Randy fell into the trap of treating all clients as equal, and in doing so failed to apply a filter. He also responded to the client's stated needs, which means he is also failing to utilise his skills as a consultant to drill deeper into the client problems to assess and then present broader strategies to demonstrate his expertise, build credibility and establish customer buy-in.

There are countless people in your market that genuinely need your help—right now! Don't waste your valuable time and energy concocting indecent proposals. Protect your valuable advice and maximise your time and resources with a tested and structured sales process.

Trust and confidence

You may have all the charismatic authority of a Hollywood actor, but that will matter little to your customers if they can't trust you. Much like being known as someone that is prepared, walks the talk and is bursting with personality, you need to be known as someone your customers can rely on when it matters most—a trusted adviser. There is a process to building trust, and if you skip a step or take your customers for granted, they will withdraw their trust from you swiftly. How trustworthy are you really? Can you build trust over a coffee or five-minute phone chat with someone you have just met? To build trust with customers, they need to have confidence in you. What is confidence? Dictionary. com says that confidence is 'Full trust; belief in the powers, trustworthiness, or reliability of a person or thing'. What a great definition and way of being to work and live by.

As a potential customer, I need to believe you will deliver on your promise. You can make the odd mistake here and there, of course, because if the customer trusts you, that's not a deal breaker. A customer needs to know you will be the first person to bring a mistake to their attention if something goes wrong, and that you won't pass the buck or, worse, blame them. You may be a tad nutty and sell the best product or service in your industry, but if you fail to build trust and deliver on your promises, your success is limited, if not ultimately lost. You must be known for being trustworthy—this has to be an element of your personal brand.

Trust builds confidence. You have to trust your process. Without confidence a salesperson is left second guessing, concocting strategies on the fly and periodically reinventing the wheel. I can tell you from experience that this is a flawed approach that breeds incompetence and underachievement. Give me a confident salesperson willing to learn and committed to never-ending improvement and I will show you a person with almost unlimited potential—competence breeds confidence.

To be confident, you need to trust what you do and sell. Too often people sell things and work for companies they don't trust. As a customer, I can smell this fear a mile off.

Can you be too confident when selling? The short answer is yes. Overconfidence is a sign of both arrogance and incompetence. It shows a lack of humility, and an unwillingness to keep learning, growing and developing skills. Overconfident people cut corners and avoid details, and also avoid being accountable when things go wrong. While confidence is essential, like most things in life, over-indulgence is ill-advised. Trust is the one single non-negotiable that transcends all relationships. Lose the trust and you lose the relationship.

Tips to build trust and confidence with customers

- Work for a company you truly believe in.
- Develop a passion for learning about what you do.
- Become an expert at delivering valuable outcomes, not excuses.
- Create successful habits around your preparation and time management.
- Exercise the power of saying no.
- Engage clients for whom you are confident you can deliver on and exceed their expectations.
- Narrow your focus and work with fewer but more valuable clients.
- Speak with your clients regularly for positive and negative feedback.

If cash flow is king, credibility is queen

Like trust, credibility can take a long time to establish, yet it can be stripped off you at light speed. I can speak from experience when I say that one erroneous move, fumble or stumble can take many years to recover from. Credibility in business is like a credit rating in your personal life. One or two black marks on your profile and no-one will take a risk on you. And why should they, if you fail to demonstrate a trustworthy past? Often businesspeople are quick to assert a sense of importance or superiority over their customers. They offer a glowing account of themselves and how adept they are at their craft.

Credibility is not something you can demand from others; like respect, it must be earned. To be credible, you must demonstrate a proven track record over an extended period in whatever it is you do. Walk the talk and make it obvious how many times your tired shoes have trodden this path. Mistakes and, more importantly, how you deal with and learn from them, also are part of the credibility-building process. In the early stages of any business, the battle with cash flow and credibility is an obvious and tiresome one. But which should you focus on achieving first?

A business can survive with strong cash flow and poor credibility, but its days are numbered and potential limited. Likewise, a company bursting with credibility won't last long without cash flow.

Both king and queen are vital to your long-term commercial success.

Use your ESP: activating your sales conversation

Selling is more than just getting customers to buy—it is the human interaction of connecting with and understanding people and then offering real solutions and choices that meet their wants and aspirations. Empathy is a compassionate understanding of the thoughts and feelings of others. Put simply, it puts you into the heart and mind of another. As a salesperson, your capacity to proactively and genuinely understand your customers, and their unique needs, challenges or desires, goes a long way to enabling you to build trust and inspire them to action. Demonstrating an empathetic and insightful understanding of your customers and what really drives and motivates them is the essence of a process I call the empathy sales process (ESP).

The ESP is a structured process that guides the conversation during the sales process (see figure 4.1). This process is a consultative approach where the focus and aim is to genuinely connect with and understand the customer's challenges and higher goals and aspirations. The solutions are then goal aligned and strategy based rather than product based, empowering the customer to make their own decisions and choose which solution is right for them.

Figure 4.1: the empathy sales process (ESP)

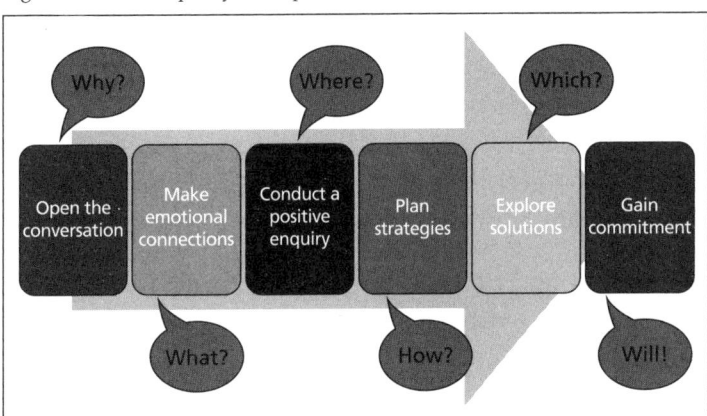

Each of the six steps of the ESP connects logically to the next, and the conversation follows a structured process to allow you to uncover the customer's needs or goals, and to discover and communicate the appropriate strategies to deliver the best solution. To make the customer feel comfortable and to avoid any misunderstandings, introduce the ESP, and make it completely transparent. You need to:

- walk the customer through what they can expect to experience to make them feel prepared and give them a sense of control over the conversation

- describe the benefits of the intended process by outlining what it means for the customer, not what it means to you

- say how long the process is likely to take based on a comparable scenario
- clearly articulate how this process will empower you to help them.

Most importantly, check that the customer is comfortable with the process that you have introduced and get their permission to proceed at each stage. A smart technique to employ after explaining how things should flow is to commence the next sentence with, 'And the benefits to you are ... '. This ensures you are consistently communicating and reinforcing the benefits for the customer.

The ESP demonstrates the power of process and will give you a tool that you can adapt and play with for your own purposes. The process always starts with a strong 'Why?' Why are you making contact? Why does this person need your help? Why are you the most qualified person to solve their problems or help them achieve their desired outcome?

Align the first step with your 'why frame'. This step is activated once you have cut through to the right person using your Red Phone technique or a similar engagement method and successfully deliver your critical piece of information. Are they a critical influencer, or a decision maker? Be sure they aren't a time-waster!

For the sake of this exercise and to demonstrate the ESP in action, let's assume you have made contact with a critical influencer via an enabler. You will therefore tailor your communication for the critical influencer, but also take into consideration the goals and desires of the decision maker. Now that you have their attention, don't disappoint and default to a self-focused stranger hell-bent on selling them something. Be sure to keep the conversation flowing forward in a meaningful direction. You must then carefully guide the customer through the sales conversation. Be wary not to skip any of the steps as you gather relevant insights and information that you can then apply to move the process forward.

Step 1: open the conversation

Right from the beginning we are working towards building a collaborative relationship with the critical influencer whereby the needs and positions of all parties, including the decision maker, are clearly defined and understood, and everyone involved shares the will to succeed. At this initial point the concepts of credibility and trust become important. Without either of these, a collaborative relationship is simply not possible. Nor is the decision maker's preference for consensus achieved. Neither credibility nor trust is given automatically: they need to be earned. Before you begin to genuinely establish credibility with your critical influencer, you must establish and clarify their objective and that of the decision maker. It is ignorant to assume that you already know this and that you have the solution in mind — if you have, it will show. You will benefit from demonstrating a genuine attempt to understand right from the word go, and begin to earn the customer's trust. First impressions last, which is why this is such a vital stage of the process to get right.

Establishing objectives upfront will not only help you keep the conversation on track, it will also allow you to check the level of buy-in and customer satisfaction at each stage of the process. In the very early stages of the relationship, your customer will determine whether they assign you an optimistic profile of credibility and trustworthiness, or a cautious profile. Minimising the differences in your communication style is one way to begin to establish an optimistic profile with your customer; the other is through highlighting your credentials to them. In a brief introduction you might describe:

- your role

- your qualifications and experience (in particular with regard to the customer's objective)

- the critical piece of information you originally communicated in your Red Phone introduction and a statement of how you intend to move forward

- the expertise of your business or your skills (in particular with regard to the customer's objective)

- how you have helped other customers in similar situations

- perhaps something personal about yourself, if it is relevant.

By establishing credibility you help to create peace of mind for the customer, and a sense that they are dealing with a person and a company that have the necessary knowledge, skills and resources to help them. This is essential when you are proactively developing relationships. An Outlaw is always outwardly focused—always looking outside themselves. However, by sharing something of yourself, such as a relevant story that informs them, or a past and relevant experience, helps you to build credibility, but you also encourage the customer to be more willing to be open about themselves and their objective.

A full analysis of your customer's current situation and their goals and aspirations will put you in a much better position. Often when a customer comes to seek out a solution, they have a greater goal or aspiration they wish to achieve or some event or transition that is happening in their life.

An effective salesperson who demonstrates empathy selling will genuinely explore what is currently happening for the customer and what they desire for the future, with the intent to help him or her to identify and clarify both their explicit and implicit needs.

Identifying *all* of the customers 'needs' in relation to their aspirations enables the salesperson to structure the most appropriate strategies for the customer whilst identifying the solutions (products and strategies) they are able to provide.

Step 2: make emotional connections

The next step in the process is driven by building emotional connections. Why is understanding emotions important here?

The age-old maxim that people buy with emotions and then rationalise their decision with logic is true. In this step your job is to understand what is really driving the customer's needs or desires and influencing their behaviour. The customer will be emotionally attached to a higher goal and aspiration, and by asking meaningful questions and applying the art of heart listening you can draw out these connections to uncover the real force behind the buying process. Once the emotional drivers and higher goals are identified, you can move to the next step of bridging the gap between the current state and the desire state.

Often, when a customer comes into an interaction with a salesperson, they start with an explicit or stated need that they require a solution for. This explicit need is usually not the real motivation for the customer to seek an interaction with us. There is often a broader underlying reason, or goal or aspiration, that motivates the customer to take action. In most cases, the customer does not disclose their underlying goal or aspiration, and in some cases they may not even recognise what this is.

When we take the time to carefully uncover and explore the customer's desired state and future goals or aspirations, we often uncover many unstated needs. In this way, the salesperson can be seen as a genuine and trusted adviser or consultant, and not just a salesperson, and the customer is clearly able to see how the solutions offered bring them closer to achieving their underlying aspirations and to identify the most appropriate strategies and solutions.

Step 3: conduct a positive enquiry

The next step in your ESP is to conduct a positive enquiry. This is achieved by asking key questions to determine the speed at which your process should move and also by asking masterful questions. This elevates you to another level of questioning that takes you beyond just information gathering to a space that allows the emergence of the goals that already have the customer's subconscious support, so they don't need to be 'sold' to the customer.

Use enquiry to encourage the customer to speculate about what it would be like to achieve their aspirations, and to express their thoughts or feelings or to evaluate, analyse or prioritise what is important to them. This facilitates an extended understanding, a deepening of context and an exploration of choices, while also connecting the customer with their subconscious desires. Where is the customer currently in regards to achieving their higher goals and aspirations? If you could wave a magic wand and grant them one wish, what would that be?

Masterful questions like these will help you get a clearer sense of where the customer is in the buying cycle. Their responses will then determine how fast or slow your process moves to the next step and beyond.

Here is an example, in which you are speaking with a critical influencer, so your questions here will relate to their time lines and the specific details of the client.

Salesperson: 'Where are you currently in terms of achieving this specific outcome?'

Customer: 'This is something we will address next year when we review our new financial year budget.'

This is a cue to slow your process down, stay connected and set an agenda for dialogue closer to the time line specified for next year. Your process stops here, for now.

Customer: 'We need this to be activated sooner rather than later, but there is no specified time frame at this stage.'

Salesperson: 'Excellent. It sounds like there is genuine need here for us to explore. I'm curious, where are you currently in the buying cycle?'

Customer: 'We are definitely in the market and have a real need for your product, but at this stage I'm just interested in a quote so I can present it to my manager [the decision maker].'

Here's where the leverage you create from your process becomes vital. In this scenario, I recommend you ask about who else is involved in the decision-making process. This is your chance to drill deeper in your positive enquiry, so you can tailor your message and ensure all key parties are being addressed in a meaningful way.

Their responses, guided by the quality of your questions, will determine how fast the process moves forward, making this stage central to your process. If you move the process forward based on the wrong information the process is rendered useless. In contrast, when you move your process forward with the right customer and right information, the process helps you and the customer move forward with greater clarity and confidence to the next step.

Step 4: plan strategies

The next step in the ESP is to identify the potential strategies that may apply to the customer.

These strategies are aimed at helping the customer achieve their goals and aspirations, and they may or may not include solutions that you are able to help them with.

By helping the customer identify strategies that both do and do not include solutions you can help them with (products or services), you demonstrate that you really are acting in their best interests as a trusted adviser.

By having the customer understand and agree with the strategies, a salesperson is far more likely to be successful when introducing solutions. There can be confusion between what constitutes a strategy and what constitutes a solution, but there should be no doubt that both should be present in your sales process.

What is a strategy? In simple terms, it's the plan. It is intended to help the customer meet their goals or fulfil their aspirations. A discussion of strategies helps the customer understand how they can move from their current situation to where they would like to be in the future.

What is a solution? It's the outcome. Once the client's need or goal has been agreed, it's up to the salesperson to identify the best potential strategies before recommending the most appropriate solution. In the ESP model, you will see that the strategies precede the solutions. A discussion about the most relevant strategies and also broader strategies (thinking beyond the scope) will help your customer understand how they can move from their current situation to where they would like to be in the future — their desired outcome.

But I regularly observe the customer determining a sales-person's process by approaching a company and asking for a solution or a price without having spent time with the salesperson collaboratively exploring the problem or gap between their current and desired states. If the salesperson responds to the customer's *stated need*, such as 'I need a quote', this does little more than incubate crazy customers and reduce the customer's buy-in. Furthermore, it shows that the salesperson is looking for quick wins rather than creating the best outcome for the customer.

As with the 99designs model, you must collaborate to innovate, and it is through this collaborative conversation that you not only gain buy-in from the customer, but are also able to tailor your strategies more accurately to the customer's solutions. Being the expert and showing a high level of skill and knowledge are critical to the Outlaw approach, but equally important is tailoring the strategy and communicating broad strategies to demonstrate your expertise and developing your reputation as a trusted adviser. When you collaborate with your customers in developing strategies, you are, by virtue of your sales process, gaining their trust and building a working relationship you can then build upon further.

Although the salesperson has so far spent considerable time understanding the customer's current situation and their future goals and aspirations, there is still one aspect that they must explore and understand: what is the customer already doing that is helping them move towards their goals and aspirations? What strategies do they themselves already have in place?

By establishing this, the salesperson can begin to identify any gaps between what the customer is doing and what they could or should be doing to help them achieve their goals.

Depending on what business the salesperson is in, these strategies may be identified in discussion with the customer, or the salesperson may need to gather all of the above information and then spend some time identifying the gaps for the customer and developing some broad strategies that may address these gaps. The salesperson will also need to identify which of these strategies they are able to support with solutions (products or services).

You should also be aware that there will be some strategies that the customer could, or should, implement that you may not be able to support them with.

If your sales process is set up correctly, there is minimal waste, as your time and resources are maximised. By not introducing solutions in this phase, you not only empower the customer with the right information to help them make the right decision, but you also demonstrate that you are acting as their trusted adviser. How important is trust in sales? It's everything! By having the customer understand and agree with the strategy, you are far more likely to be successful when you introduce the solution. And if possible *avoid* recommending only one solution. Instead propose options and give your customer a choice. Why? So they can make the buying decision and own it.

Step 5: explore solutions

This step in the ESP is aimed at providing the customer with more specific information about how the salesperson can help them achieve their goals. The objective is to assist the customer in making an informed decision and owning the buying process. The salesperson takes the opportunity to convey benefit-oriented information to the customer about the recommended solutions, allowing the customer to then decide on the option(s) that are right for them.

The point at which the salesperson introduces solutions can be a major determinant in how the customer responds. At this stage of the sales process, the salesperson should be discussing overall possible solutions in terms of benefits rather than the specific product or service details or features.

We aim first to gain the customer's interest in and agreement on the solution(s), and then we may move on to an explanation of the solution's features. We gain the customer's attention and interest by clearly positioning the 'What's in it for me?' for the customer through using benefit language.

If a salesperson describes a product or service feature without describing the corresponding benefits, the customer may not understand how the solution will add value for them. They may not understand the 'So what?' for them.

The features of a solution will remain consistent from customer to customer; however, benefits are tailored to the customer's goals or aspirations. By linking solutions directly to the customer's goals and aspirations, the customer will be more engaged in the solutions and less likely to raise concerns or objectives, particularly ones related to price. Any perceived negatives from the customer's perspective will be outweighed by the perceived value of the benefits the solution will add. If the salesperson has done a thorough job when determining the customer's goals and aspirations, he or she should have identified what is important to the customer.

In discussing solutions with the customer, the salesperson can demonstrate value to the customer by relating not just the specific product or service benefits, but also the higher level strategy. This way the customer can clearly see how the solution helps them move toward their goals and aspirations.

Remember: always describe the solution(s) in benefit-oriented language.

Step 6: gain commitment

The success the salesperson has had in implementing the previous steps will have a large impact on the response the customer has to this step of the sales process. Assuming that the previous steps have been positive, this step should really feel and sound like a natural conclusion to the conversation for the customer. It is, however, the salesperson's responsibility to actively initiate this aspect of the sales process. Unfortunately, many salespeople feel uncomfortable actively asking for the business (as you will learn when you meet Gun Shy Gary in chapter 6). Many of the reasons that a salesperson is reluctant to ask for the business can be eliminated by:

- seeking commitment to proceed throughout the sales conversations, and gaining the right to proceed from one step to the next
- recognising the appropriate point in the conversation to ask for the commitment
- identifying the level of commitment the customer is willing to give at that point.

Once the buying signals have been identified the salesperson needs to take action. The action should reflect whether the customer is giving the green, amber or red signal and should not necessarily be asking for the business as this stage.

It is at this point that customers are most likely to raise a concern or objection, or express their reluctance to make a commitment to buy, although this can happen at any point in the sales process. If the salesperson has been carefully observing the buying signals, they will be aware that these concerns or objections are coming.

Concerns are not necessarily an indication that the customer is not satisfied with your strategies or solutions: they are often just another way the customer expresses their needs. In fact, expressing concern may very well be an indication that they are ready to buy. However, if the salesperson has not understood the customer's goals and aspirations fully, or has not demonstrated value sufficiently, legitimate objections are more likely to surface here.

The way the salesperson handles the concern or objection will have a significant impact on whether the customer decides to buy or not. Here are some tips for managing the customer's concerns and objections:

- Don't become defensive or get into a debate — this will only put the customer offside.

- Don't overwhelm the customer with further information in an attempt to justify your recommendations. Simply be concise and clear about how your recommendations will help the customer achieve their goals or aspirations. This may not have been clear enough initially.

- If the salesperson hasn't fully understood the customer's needs and goals, a legitimate concern may arise. By clarifying this need or goal and genuinely responding to it, the salesperson may strengthen their connection and likelihood of gaining commitment.

By effectively utilising gain-agreement techniques, the salesperson will appear confident, and this confidence will project onto the customer. To retain this image of confidence, the salesperson must give the customer comfortable space to consider the commitment without interruption.

This is not the time to introduce new information, which might only confuse the customer. Unfortunately this is exactly what nervous salespeople do. Allowing space for the customer to consider the commitment means the customer will either raise additional concerns, which you can effectively address, or agree to the commitment.

End the conversation but stay connected

To help alleviate any anxiety or uncertainty for the customer, the salesperson should always end the sales conversation in a positive manner, which communicates to the customer that the relationship is more than just the sale. It is important for the salesperson to indicate that they will be a partner in this relationship, both now and in the future and to map out the next steps clearly.

Maybe means no

Irrespective of whether you are working to a tested process or not, many salespeople still never get to hear the word no. Instead they get the insidious response of maybe. This could be evidence you are entertaining the crazies, but it could also mean your process needs refinement. One of your jobs as a salesperson is to circumvent the murky fog of maybe and to uncover either a yes or a no. There are, of course, exceptions to every rule, but no should mean no, and in my world maybe also means no.

Chasing dead-ends is a waste of time and energy. Sure, play the numbers and the law of averages, but you're better served focusing your time and energy chasing the beautiful sound of yes. Trust your process. There are customers out there ready to buy from you right now, but you won't have much time or energy left to find them if you're too busy chasing maybes.

Leverage is key to hearing the word yes, and leverage is born of process. You also need to give your customers a meaningful and compelling reason to buy from you. Like Randy the IT consultant who is too easily aroused, any salesperson can conduct meaningless meetings, write proposals and put a cost estimate together. That's easy, particularly when your boss is paying you to do it, yet fewer salespeople can call themselves masters of getting a yes.

Ineffective salespeople seldom have the appropriate leverage to create the right buying decision, they simply present their case and hope for the best, hearing responses from clients such as, 'We'll think about it.' Or 'Thanks for that, I'll need to review and I'll come back to you.' These two statements and others like them are crushing blows to a salesperson, but they are all too common for the average ones.

If a client says no, at least you know where you stand and you don't have to submit yourself to the months of following up emails and borderline harassment calls. And if you have done your job properly, which is always to facilitate the right outcome for your customer, you have the confidence to know that there is nothing else to say but yes or no.

This is the type of conviction and confidence you should have as a successful salesperson. Winning salespeople are clear and concise: grey is their enemy and so is the word maybe. If you are working to your tested process and know you have followed it correctly and achieved the customer's buy-in along the way, there is no guesswork. The grey will more often than not be replaced by the word yes.

Are you sure you don't want fries with that?

We all know up-selling is an important element of any process, once we have achieved a level of commitment, but what is the concept of down-selling? Down-selling is the art of narrowing a customer's expectations and matching them more effectively with a solution that best fulfils their needs or desires. Too often I see salespeople preying on their customer's ignorance by up-selling them, even when no extra value is being created for the customer. The salesperson is simply feeding their own agenda and getting the customer to pay for it. This is the power of process in action. Unfortunately salespeople who understand its influence can harness it for the wrong reasons, to the customer's detriment.

Following is an example of how a salesperson's greed and failure to align his solution with my genuine need cost him not only the business but the ongoing relationship. When I was searching for a new office, I dealt with a salesperson at a leasing company who tried diligently to persuade me to pay for a much larger office space, with more features, than I needed. He was communicating a broader strategy, but his options were not relevant or feasible. I explained on numerous occasions what my very specific needs were, but they seemed to take backseat to the salesperson's own needs. I asked the salesperson in a curious tone, 'What would you do if you were me in this situation?' He responded with conviction, 'I would definitely take larger office space, just in case you need the extra features down the track.' He then proceeded to tell me (again) about the benefits of all the (non-relevant) extra features, as if to smokescreen his response in the hope I would lose my better judgement and simply agree to the contract terms.

This is a classic example of a salesperson demonstrating a complete disregard for what is really important to the customer. Had this salesperson *truly* listened to me he would have provided me with an opportunity to buy in, and increased the likelihood of making the sale. Instead he went for an irrelevant up-sell without first establishing my trust or my buy-in, and in doing so he lost the potential of winning more business downstream when my needs better matched his value. He has also lost any chance of my providing him with goodwill and referrals.

McDonald's has built a fast-food empire on convenience, average food, smart process and, of course, up-selling. But when you drive through a McDonald's and a service attendant asks you, 'Would like to upsize your meal?' and you respond, 'No, thank you,' they don't reply with, 'Are you sure? I mean really sure?' They listen and then act accordingly. Up-selling is a powerful skill, but only when your customer is getting more value, not less. Build trust and demonstrate you are acting in your customer's best interests, and then up-sell by creating more value. To sell more you always have to deliver more.

Leading the process

Outlaws are on the edge, constantly pushing the boundaries to improve and gain an advantage. Competitive by nature, they hate to lose. Every opportunity is a chance to express their skills and commitment to their cause. They value their time and take what they do seriously. For an Outlaw their role is more than a job: they consider it a body of work. Include just a few of these high performers in a sales team and align them with the right process and you will see any business radically transform. So how do you develop and support your core sales team so they evolve into sales leaders?

Every sales team should have critical insights and a clear view of what success looks like. Building a success profile is essential for determining a framework of what capabilities, skills and behaviours you need to nurture, encourage and replicate. This serves as a blueprint to grow and develop your team. It forms a foundation from which to establish a proficiency pathway to achieve enhanced time to competence and success.

What strikes me most about Outlaws is the way they operate. Their approach seldom seems rigid, instead it's more fluid and natural. They do work to a trusted process, like the ESP, but they tailor where necessary. Most have a natural creative flare that allows them to communicate the bigger picture and tell a compelling story. Others are deeply analytical and walk to a structured beat. And there are, of course, the instinctive entrepreneurs who embrace risk and see things through the prism of opportunity. Being an Outlaw is not restricted to a certain personality type — anyone can be an Outlaw if they apply a certain mindset and skills. How do you harness these innate characteristics and effectively incorporate them into the trusted method? The most effective approach is to exploit these natural traits and ensure the model is fluid enough to accommodate them. The less successful will invariably under-utilise their intrinsic talents, failing to identify what they can develop to align to the profile of success.

Call to sales leaders

To get the best from your sales team often means letting some of them go, and if you're really honest, perhaps most of them. Take a blowtorch to your low performers, particularly those who fail to adopt and adapt your trusted process, and don't demonstrate a willingness to learn and keep growing. Let them fail somewhere else or at your competitors' expense. The middle band, just under your high-performance category, has the highest growth potential. To develop these people means getting clear on your success profile and identifying any capability and experience gaps for development as they work via the process. From there you can establish a clear proficiency pathway that develops these capabilities and provides relevant experiences to ensure the opportunity for success is fast-tracked. This development pathway is supported by ongoing coaching and relevant on-the-job opportunities for salespeople to practise the process.

As for your current HiPer-salespeople, keep challenging them! They will demand higher mountains to climb, so inspire them. They are often unique characters, so be sure to acknowledge their capabilities and reward their unique contributions. They often see and approach things differently from most, and that's what makes them so valuable. What may seem strange to others works for them—harness it!

☞ Action points ☜

- Process is the mother of replication. Develop your six-step ESP and replicate the desired outcome time and again.

- Attack time-wasters before they attack you.

- Collaborate to innovate and inspire greater levels of buy-in from both team members and customers.

- Trust in yourself and in your process: you may get it wrong occasionally, but in the end you will be miles ahead.

CHAPTER 5

IGNITE THE PASSION CONTAGION

There is no passion to be found playing small—in settling for a life that is less than the one you are capable of living.

Nelson Mandela, anti-apartheid and civil rights leader

Outlaws follow a career they are passionate about. They understand there are demands and responsibilities in life, but they don't sacrifice their values for an unfulfilled existence.

Life is a precious gift that is often taken for granted. Your time is way too valuable and transient to waste on people or a career that isn't truly meaningful to you. Here's an interesting fact: the average life expectancy of a Western male is around 77 years and for females it's a tad higher. We don't grace this Earth for long: the proverbial clock is ticking, so if you're not passionate about what you do, what are you waiting for?

Reading your passion meter

To be the best you can be at what you do, you need to stick at it long enough to develop the specialist skills to master it. In addition, if you're working every day in a passionless state, the rest of your life, including your family, is affected, so what's the real cost?

When you meet a person full of passion, you will notice that *what* they say is always less important than *how* they say it. If you can't get excited about what you sell, then at the very least get excited about how you sell it! My old mentor Big Kev's tag line was 'I'm excited!' At the conclusion of every infomercial he sprayed these passionate words at the television screen. These words were not just heard from his lips — they jolted his entire body. That's the type of passion and conviction you must demonstrate when you sell. If you don't do that now, ask yourself why not. Perhaps you're in the wrong job. Are you frustrated by a lack of support? Are you being bullied by teammates? Not being valued? Do you want to be inspired, instead of managed? Or maybe you're focusing on the wrong things, instead of grabbing life by the scruff and pursuing a career that is truly meaningful to you.

What you do in life says a lot more about you than anything you can ever say. By following a career that you are truly passionate about, by default you inspire others to do it too! Where you find passion, you will also find meaning. Passion is so important because it usually oozes out of every pore. Passionate people are never the passengers.

I love being around passionate people: these luminous individuals emit a highly flammable energy and seem to enjoy life and get more of out of everyday situations. We all know what happens once passion leaves the building. We usually leap head first out the window after it! Passion is a life force, it can move mountains. Passion has the power to transcend and transform. It can pick you up if you have been knocked down. It will inspire you when no-one else will. Passion will keep you up at night as you ponder the fruits it may bring you. And maybe, just maybe, passion will find you, and when it does you will know about it! Passion is beautiful. Passion is creative. Passion is intense. Passion is loving. Passion is full on! Passion is sensitive. Passion is contagious.

However, passion has a nasty little sister called reckless. She is impetuous by nature and acts purely on impulse. She is made of pure passion: the unbridled and unadulterated kind. She has the power to win and influence all in her way. She is intoxicating, sultry and seductive. Equally smart and sexy! You just can't get enough. But don't be fooled: her allure is a wicked facade. Reckless is self-centred, indulgent and in constant need of instant gratification. She skilfully gets her own way, even if it means throwing you into harm's way. She is selfish and can never be trusted. If you don't tame passion you will soon meet reckless. Many successful people have been seduced by reckless, jumping into hot deep pools of passion without testing the waters. Tame your passion and let it serve you rather than work against you. Sometimes you need to bring things back a peg or two and talk them through, and then proceed slowly and cautiously. No harm in that. Some say passion is the secret to success; I say that's only in part true. Passion must be tamed because reckless is dying to meet you.

Passion meter activity

On a scale of 1–10, with 10 being the highest, rate your level of passion towards your role over the past month. Got a number? Okay. The second part of this activity is to recall a time in your career when you were most passionate. Take yourself back to a time and place when your passion level was huge, say an 8 or above. What were you doing? Where were you? Why were you so aroused? What was it that unlocked so much passion? And then ask yourself, what's stopping you from being in that place again?

People often mistake a lack of results for a lack of passion. Often the passion is still there, in a dark and dormant state, until a certain level of success is realised. Don't fall into this trap: work hard to unlock the passion even when you're not succeeding. This is vital for maintaining your motivation levels and ensuring you can stick long enough to improve and keep growing in confidence and competence. Sometimes life throws us things that de-motivate us, and our passion meter reading drops. That's okay, just don't resign to it: keep fighting. Focus on things you are passionate about—perhaps your passion is not work related. That's okay, too, just be sure to switch the passion on when you need to.

Maybe you're just not passionate about what you're doing or selling. Perhaps a pay packet is the only reason you're doing it. If so, take that as a cue to move on to something that really turns you on.

Equally important is surrounding yourself with other passionate people. You then feed off each other's energy. Passion is highly contagious, so offer your passion to others when they are flat, and look for passion in others when you are down. Passion is energy, just as it is a mindset. Your health is also a key ingredient in maintaining a high level of passion. Stay healthy and focused on the end game. Give me a passionate salesperson and I'll show you passionate customers.

Never sell a carrot to a rabbit

Why? Rabbits love carrots and they are the most discerning of carrot connoisseurs, and it's almost guaranteed they know more about carrots than you do. So if you're selling carrots to a rabbit, you're at a distinct disadvantage, especially when you lack a genuine passion for your product. There is nothing more disempowering than selling to a customer who has more passion for, and a deeper understanding of, your product than you. These customers can see things from a higher vantage point. The rabbit will know the finer details about carrots, like where to find more of them, what constitutes quality and how value is best measured. They will also have a broader context as well as meaningful experiences to draw upon regarding their most precious resource. Knowledge is a form of influence and power, particularly when you are buying, as it creates leverage.

When you are selling a carrot to a rabbit, you had better have, at the very least, as much passion about what you're selling as the rabbit has in buying it. Fail to take a genuine interest in your product and reflect an equal level of expertise, and you will come across as ignorant, lacking credibility and uninspiring. If you can't match them in these areas, you're not contributing to the conversation or influencing their behaviour.

If there's no way you can converse intellectually with the rabbit, be sure to bring another rabbit in with you. This is most common in tech and high-end solution selling, where the specialist skills required for hunting for new business parts ways with the ability to process and articulate complexity. Rabbits aren't that complex, but when it comes to carrots they really know their stuff. Demonstrate your appreciation for them by loving what you sell by drawing out their opinions and positive experiences and acknowledging their own expertise. Genuinely mirror their passion and enthusiasm. When you achieve this, you won't need to sell the carrot—the rabbit will sell it to you.

Curiouser and curiouser!

Lewis Carroll, *Alice in Wonderland*

What's the big idea?

A lot of people are searching for the next big idea. When a phenomenon like Facebook hits, the herd reacts and curves in perfect formation, in pursuit with mouths salivating in anticipation of cashing in big time. If the explosion is loud enough, it can be heard by all, with people rallying from all parts of the world to emulate it, but by then it's too late.

When you try imitating a big idea all you're doing is chasing someone else's dream—there's nothing inspiring about that. It will also mean you are focusing too much on things that are constantly changing instead of long-lasting, and often you will miss what's right in front of you. Like the stuff people wanted 10 years ago and will still want 10 years on. I'm talking about speedy service, friendly staff, a personal touch, guarantees, accountability, prompt responses to problems, and, of course, value for money.

Of course you should innovate and drive change, but make sure your big idea focuses on and enhances the things that matter most to your customers, the things that don't change that much, and you will hit the mark with customers more often. Our world is forever changing, and what's hot today will be tepid tomorrow. Instead of chasing the next big idea, start focusing more on the smaller, simpler and less sensational things, as these are the things that invariably matter most: your customers. This is the best place to start. And from there the dream may just turn into a reality.

I dream for a living.

Steven Spielberg, award-winning film director

The curse of complacency

Being competent at what you do is a start, but it's not enough if you want to be world class. People who stay competent long enough kill long-term personal and company value. That may seem a harsh and sweeping statement, but competence breeds complacency, which leads to mediocrity. To be an Outlaw you will need to develop your knowledge and capabilities to take you beyond being competent to being the best you can be at what you do.

How does *your* best benefit your customers? It means they get the best person for the job, who provides the best advice, commitment to outcomes, and value for their risk and investment. Ask yourself, can you be the best at what you do? If not, why not? Who is the best and are they someone you can learn from? If they are a competitor, apply your filter to determine if they are closed and aggressive, passive and indifferent, or open and collaborative. There's a lot to learn from competitors. Another way to look at being the best is to consider what can you be the best at, and can you commercialise that? This may be something that you have never tried, but have a natural flair for. You will never know until you give it a go. I am not suggesting that this process is easy, but resigning to a life of competence will ultimately prove much harder, marked as it is with the bitter zest of regret. There's no passion in that.

I regularly get requests from inspired and sometimes desperate businesspeople wanting to partner on a business idea. When evaluating any proposition like this, I start by getting to know the person behind the idea. It's the people behind a business that make it truly unique and successful, but not just any old competent people, the right people. The best people are always self-motivated and disciplined—sure, the passion is there, but they are also willing to get their hands dirty and have plenty of skin in the game. They are committed to learning and self-improvement. The best people have a vision and they stick at it until the job is done. And the best people always attract like-minded people. To be an Outlaw is not necessarily being the best now, but it is a commitment to being the best and being willing to stick until you realise it.

On the other hand, competent people do their job well, but doing it well is all they will ever do. Being the best you can be may take you a lifetime to achieve. But that's fine, because you're following a path that lights up every molecule of your being and the reward is not just being the best, but the journey itself. Life is way too short to be competent and live without passion.

How to pump a flat dream

When a team is flat and lacking in passion, this is usually an indication of deflated leadership. When the team's energy levels are low and the individuals within the team are not getting the desired results, they feel devalued. The passion been sucked right out of them. The first thing you need to do is try to pump the deflated team with some passion and energy. Tools down for a moment! As a sales leader your mission now is to reignite the passion and get your team to buy into their role and the ways they uniquely contribute to the success of the business. This can be achieved by setting up regular collaborative sessions or team meetings that allows all team members to voice their opinions on the team's performance and for each person to put all the concerns, issues and challenges on the table. Especially on where they feel they personally add the most value to the business and how much time they are spending in that activity. From here you can integrate their feedback and align their time with the activities that allow them to produce the most value.

Ask the team members to measure their level of passion on the passion meter. Follow this up with another request to help them to move their level of passion up the passion meter scale. How you do this will vary from person to person. This is where your leadership skills and your ability to lead by example come in, and you can show them what's possible so they can really sink their teeth into it.

This isn't always a pleasant exercise, and some people just aren't built to fit the role, so exercise the power of saying no by challenging them in new ways or moving them on. In any case, having these challenging conversations is nothing compared with the frustrations attached to letting the situation continue untreated. Once all the challenges and each person's real value are identified, you can move the team forward through structured and specific training and development to further enhance their skills and capabilities. In most cases, team members simply want to be heard and appreciated. They also want to see what's possible and know that their fearless leader cares enough to understand the unique ways they contribute to the business. And remember that, as a leader, if you are asking your team to take on constructive feedback, you must also demonstrate this ability yourself.

Is your loyalty program loyal to your customers?

In stark contrast to the flower lady who inspired me with her passion and personality (see chapter 3), here's a story that demonstrates how easy it can be to lose a loyal customer—forever.

I made a reservation to stay at a five-star hotel in Darling Harbour, Sydney. The booking was for the coming Friday. However, to my surprise on the Sunday the week before my booking, I received a survey email from the hotel's parent company asking to rate my stay. Perplexed, I rang them back and quoted my membership number. I asked why this email had been sent to me, given I was due to stay the following week? Their response stunned me.

The customer support person stated in a confident tone that the booking was complete. I explained the booking was for the following Friday. To my amazement, he disagreed. He then put me on hold and came back a minute or so later. He scoffed, 'The booking was for the previous day and that had now passed. I'm sorry but there is nothing we can do as your credit card has been processed. He then suggested I call the hotel directly to see if they could resolve the matter. I rang the hotel, only to receive the same robotic and emotionless response from their manager. I quizzed the manager: did he sincerely believe it was okay to take my money with no exchange of services? His response was a pause, followed by a shallow, 'I'm sorry, but there is nothing we can do but offer you a small discount on a future stay.' This irritated me, particularly given I'm a loyalty club member and a frequent visitor to their hotels.

I sliced my loyalty card into pieces and lobbed it straight into the bin, taking my loyalty for this company with it.

As customers, we carefully choose who we will give our loyalty to, and always look for evidence that we are being genuinely valued. I was once loyal to this hotel chain and provided my loyalty by staying with them regularly all over the world. Yet they didn't honour my commitment when it mattered most to me. I have moved on and know someone else will appreciate my business. Loyalty is a two-way street: if you want your customers to be loyal to you, give them a good reason to be.

Take it personally

When you're passionate about what you do, you're well within your rights to take it personally when someone lets you down. As my hotel story shows, your passionate customers sure do—and so should you. High-performance salespeople invest most of their time during the week growing and developing their business, and improving their craft, which often spills over into the wee hours and weekends. If you're an Outlaw your business is not just a job: it represents a significant part of who you are as a person.

In your travels, from time to time you will cross paths with a customer who lacks a legitimate passion for what they do. They don't have a duty of care to honour vendor relationships and couldn't care less about you—you're just a lowly salesperson. Their core purpose every week is to simply grind through it with their sanity intact. Don't take their lack of passion as a reflection of you, but take it personally when a customer lets you down or breaks their promise. If you devote not only your time but also a significant portion of *yourself* to every opportunity and a customer is willing to take that but can't even take 30 seconds from their day to respond or cut you loose, this says a lot about their character. You're probably better off without customers like these.

Outlaws take it personally, and that's exactly what I look for in HiPer-salespeople. These people work with passion and sprinkle bits of themselves into all of their activities. They work hard and expect high standards of themselves and others. There's nothing wrong with that. Don't let a passionless customer affect your attitude or determine your behaviour. You're better than that! If you're going to invest a hefty percentage of your life in a chosen field, for goodness sake, take it personally! And when a customer lets you down, don't let it fester: move on and contribute to someone else who deserves it.

> *The law is reason, free from passion.*
>
> Aristotle, ancient Greek philosopher

A cure for the common culture

One person fighting for a cause is powerful; a group of people united with a purpose and fighting for the same cause is called a revolution. Forming a team of like-minded people can be tricky, but when you get it right, your business may reach spectacular heights through the success of only a handful of people.

Before creating a successful team, however, you need to have at least one exceptional person you can use as a role model. Someone has to go there first! Whether this is a company founder or a senior leader, or a gun for hire, there must be a working and best-practice process and way of being for you to replicate. Once you have a HiPer-salesperson whose core characteristics and behaviours you can model, then form the blueprint of your team, keeping in mind that it's acceptable to have varying personalities in the same team—this enables your team members to demonstrate versatility and engage a broader market. You don't need to literally clone team members to replicate successfully, but they must all have, at the very least, what I call attributes that cure the common culture.

Charisma and confidence

Your ability to be yourself and engage people and make them feel important is part of your cause as an Outlaw. There is a lot to be said for confidence in any area of life. In business, if you're not confident you will struggle to gain any real buy-in and trust from others. Customers will sense your lack of confidence in either your own ability or what you're selling. When your customers smell fear, this makes it almost impossible for you to gain their trust and lead them successfully to the desired outcome.

Commonality and cohesion

We naturally trust people that validate who we are—our beliefs, values and opinions. We usually go to great lengths to surround ourselves with liked-minded people, including team members. The most successful teams I have been involved with share their ideas willingly and opinions constructively and work together towards common goals bound by common values.

Capability and commitment

You have to know your stuff, be a rabbit and strive to be the best. Invariably, capability derives from taking a genuine interest in what you are doing, and a commitment to stick with it long enough until you're good, and then hopefully exceptional, at it. You may be able to look the part and talk it up with the best of them, but if you consistently let people down and break promises, it's only a matter of time before your incompetence catches up with you. This all makes setting up and developing an inspiring sales culture critical to any business.

Contributing to the cause

In business if you aren't contributing you're either doing nothing or you're taking from others. Many people think selling is the art of getting what you want: this is only partly true. The real movers and shakers understand how contribution serves themselves and others.

We all know people in life who just take, so as we get older and wiser we tend not to associate with these people for too long. Perhaps if we are really honest with ourselves, we take more than we give sometimes, too. And this is easy to do, particularly when we get desperate. Over the years, I've been desperate more than once, so I can speak from experience when I say, no one likes a desperado.

When we are really needy we think we don't have much choice other than to take. But we do have a choice. When you don't have much, this is the best time to give. Give more passion! More energy! More value. Too often I see salespeople contracting when they are faced with challenges, instead of expanding and meeting their challenge head on.

Contributing can be boiled down to a simple definition: always go the extra mile!

Do all the little things that add value, beyond the usual. That doesn't need to cost you money or drain your energy—just do something small and make it a big habit. Little things mean a lot. A pat on the back. A smile or a cheeky wink. A thank you. A joke. Be positive to be around. Be interested. Ask questions and really listen to the answers. It's not hard. The little things add up over time.

It's never crowded along the extra mile.

Dr Wayne Dyer, international best-selling author

Good isn't good enough

Mamma owns a Malaysian restaurant. The food is reasonably priced and always tasty. When I ring to place my order I am always greeted passionately by the owner. Mamma has a minuscule, bird-like frame, a glowing complexion and is always bursting with energy. Her every sentence ends with the loving words, 'Okay, darling.' When I arrive at her restaurant, she greets me with a warm smile and asks me how I am. She then offers me something extra for free or just throws it in anyway without telling me. I pay, and then she scampers around the counter, puckers her big red lips and plants a wet one on my cheek! And I love every minute of it.

I always leave Mamma's restaurant feeling noticeably more positive than when I walked in. In fact, Mamma makes my experience memorable and meaningful. The exchange of money seems insignificant. However, as I head home, my positive thoughts deteriorate to a sense of disappointment. You see, her restaurant is never busy. Most times when I go there the shop has maybe one or two tables full, and the rest of the restaurant is empty. I just know it's only a matter of time before she is gone. This troubles me. The woman is a real gem—and she is the exception, not the rule. So full of love and passion, and her food is delicious to boot. Yet, she is never busy. This shouldn't make sense, but sadly it does.

Passion on its own is not enough to succeed. It's a start, but that's all it is. You need a process of attracting, engaging and leading customers to the win–win outcome. And the passion for the product or service you sell then contributes to your customers' coming back again and again, and bringing friends. Mamma's restaurant is situated in a run-down old strip of shops directly across from an old petrol station. She has no pedestrian traffic and is situated in a part of town that is no longer fashionable. Mamma does no marketing and hasn't developed a way of proactively developing new relationships. She is not getting enough customers through her door to give her the goodwill traction she needs as word of mouth spreads. She is also not adept at social marketing, which is something she needs to help spread the word in her local area. She is doing some things right by delivering more value, but that's not enough. There are new retail strips and restaurants springing up like weeds around her and in better traffic areas. Mamma must move with the times in order to grow and drive change and progress forward, or she is out of business. This is a harsh reality for Mamma, so she must acknowledge and embrace it or her little restaurant will be no more than a bitter-sweet memory.

Harley-Davidson

Harley-Davidson is an iconic brand that has stood the test of time. The product really hasn't changed that much in more than 100 years, which is an extraordinary feat in itself. What's more, it's a brand, much like Apple, that inspires fierce customer loyalty. In fact, the Harley customer is more like a cult follower. What other brand can you think of that moves their customer so deeply that they are compelled to decorate themselves in tattoos to celebrate their passion for the brand?

The Harley-Davidson statement of vision for the company gives you a sense of what the brand really represents in the hearts and minds of their customers:

> We fulfil dreams inspired by the many roads of the world by providing remarkable motorcycles and extraordinary customer experiences. We fuel the passion for freedom in our customers to express their own identity.

What an inspiring vision! I regularly challenge my clients, no matter what industry they are in, to think about their mission and to draw inspiration from Harley-Davidson. When you have passionate customers, as Harley-Davidson does, you don't need to change your product that much. Instead, you will need to honour your promise and never compromise your brand values for short-term gains. If you want to take your customer on a long ride of passion you will need to understand what turns them on and then keep delivering it. There is more to the Harley story than appears on the surface. Here are some more interesting elements that help to foster the cult-like behaviour in these customers:

- *Harlean.* A language that consists of technical jargon you will hear at a H.O.G. (see below) chapter gathering. Essentially only lingo and terminology a Harley rider will understand.

- *The secret wave.* Is it the middle finger? I will leave that for you to explore.

- *Tattoos.* This is absurd really; rarely does a product evoke this type of behaviour.

- *Customers pay more for branded accessories.* This demonstrates the brand's real value in the hearts and minds of customers.

- *Freedom, tribal and belonging.* Harley is more than a brand: it's a way of life.

- *H.O.G. (Harley Owners Groups) Chapters.* When challenged by the Japanese motorcycle manufacturers, Harley almost went under. Despite having no marketing budget, the company rebuilt the profile of the brand through H.O.G. chapter meetings, where riders from all over America and now globally, meet to share ideas, stories and their passion.

- *Loud and raw.* The brand has a distinctive sound that resonates with its customers—that will never change.

These are some of the characteristics that make Harley-Davidson an Outlaw. The brand defies the rules of conventional brand wisdom, in that it hasn't needed to evolve or change that much in over 100 years, and has remained true to what it means to its customers. The product also gives customer much more than a transaction: the product represents a way of life and has a strong influence over the customer's behaviour. A secret language, paying more for branded products and tattoos are all signs of a deeply connected and passionate customer. Would your customers tattoo your logo on their butts?

It's time to get passionate!

Sales is a game, though not always the numbers game that some would suggest—it's more of a mental game. Every year, I work with hundreds of salespeople across a broad range of industries. What strikes me most is the chasm between the high and low performers. This distinction is always a matter of mindset and measured by a deep passion for success. If you haven't made a sale in a few weeks, or heaven forbid months, you should be anxious. That state should change to frustration and, if that persists, then raw anger! By anger, I don't mean slapping customers in the face until they buy. I refer to a deep sense of injustice for not succeeding at what you do that transforms into action and results. This sensation is essential to all creatures that compete for survival in any jungle. Despite modern advances, human beings are still primitive creatures. Just tune into the six o'clock news of an evening and you'll get a taste of reality. We live in a ruthless world and occasionally things don't go our way. Understand this, and then swiftly get over it. When your back is to the wall, slowly stretch your fingers and spread your claws—get angry!

Businesspeople often blame their lack of performance on external forces, such as market conditions, ineffective marketing, dealing with too many time-wasters, or a crackpot manager. They curse, bicker and spit at others with resentment. These people are angry all right, but their energy is directed at everyone but themselves. The first person you need to confront is you! Look yourself dead in the eye and demand answers! And it's the answers you're most reluctant to acknowledge that move you forward.

Are you lazy? Fearful of rejection? Not willing to do the hard yards? Are you too focused on money? Does your ego need a stroke? Are you caught up in internal politics? Is your confidence shot? Are you exhausted? Do you feel unloved? Do you lack passion? Okay. So what?

Don't put your own story above the need to get the job done. Turn your anger into action, and your action into passion. Pick up the Red Phone and make that big, bold call! In that big presentation today, take control, be assertive, use your ESP and then ask for the business! Stop fluffing around the edges and cut through to the outcome. Making mistakes is okay, provided you keep learning and keep going! You may be down now, but never be down for long. If you're in sales, you're paid to sell. If you can't and won't do that, then move on and find a role more aligned with your natural skills and cerebral capacity. If your passion isn't there, go find it. When push comes to shove, you're the only person who can change your reality. Yes, at times it's a nasty, scary and unforgiving jungle out there, so start channelling your passion. Don't get eaten — get passionate!

☞ **Action points** ✍

- Use the passion meter regularly to assess your level of passion and work towards moving it up the scale. Tame your passion, but know when to turn it on!

- Surround yourself with passionate people; share your passion with others; and go looking for it when you don't have it.

- Good isn't good enough: be the best you can be by following a career you're passionate about!

- Sell with passion and you create passionate customers. So much so they may just tattoo your logo on their butts!

CHAPTER 6

INFLUENCE WITH A DIFFERENCE

It takes tremendous discipline to control the influence, the power
you have over other people's lives.

Clint Eastwood, actor and film director

'Let there be light!' boomed the bold voice from deep within the darkness.

Silence followed for what seemed like an eternity—until a careful voice echoed back from the dark shadows: 'Why do we need light?'

God pondered the careful voice for some time before offering a reply. And it was from this enlightening exchange that the first-ever sales pitch was born. Light soon followed.

Nothing gets done without some selling first.

We all sell something, whether we acknowledge it or not. Sometimes the sell is subconscious and other times it's more overt. This could mean selling yourself on why something or someone is truly important to you? Perhaps it's selling your kids on the perils of drug use before the local drug dealer sells to them first? Or maybe it's selling yourself on why you shouldn't raid the fridge late at night. In any case, we are always selling or being influenced by someone or something. How we influence ourselves and enrol others in our vision or values determines the mark we leave on the world.

We are most influential and more persuasive when what we sell makes a difference and changes the way others think and behave. Think of some of the world's most notable Outlaws who left an indelible mark on society, including Mahatma Gandhi, Martin Luther King Jr, John Lennon, Charles Darwin and Nelson Mandela. These are just some of the bold and virtuous Outlaws who throughout history sold their vision. They defied the rules and threw themselves into harm's way to fight for what they believed in. When you sell with this much passion and conviction you become unstoppable, and your vision resonates long after you are gone. As an Outlaw your primary objective is to help your customers realise more: more value, more benefits, and more potential.

You may not be here to change the world, and you may not want to, and that's fine, but you better know how to get what you want or you will forever be forced to live in a state of need.

Every day Outlaws sell themselves on:

- why they need to get out of bed with a spring in their step
- why they won't let challenges and setbacks consume them
- why their customers will buy from them and not their competitors
- why they will ultimately succeed, no matter what.

As an Outlaw you choose to travel the path less travelled, in many ways carving your own path and charting a more purposeful course. This journey takes courage and determination; you will have doubts from time to time and face challenges that seem insurmountable. You will question your nerve and capabilities, but that's only natural. If you truly want it, you will fight for it.

The sell always starts with a meaningful 'why?' Your 'why frame' gives you purpose. It should then flow through your Arc of Influence gaining momentum as it reaches and continues through your ESP. By the time your why has reached this point, it will have increased in clarity and potency. Be mindful that without a strong why and an ability to communicate with purpose no-one will buy. Similarly, if you can't first sell yourself on why your customer will buy from you, why should they buy from you?

The wild, wild East

Often a sale will come down to a final negotiation where two parties aim to draw a sales conversation to a conclusion. As you may recall, this sixth step of your ESP is referred to as the gain agreement phase. In old school sales vernacular this is commonly referred to as closing the sale. This phase of the process has always been considered the most critical step. However, if you set up your process correctly and trust in it, this step will be the smoothest and require the least amount of stress and time, because it is a simple and logical next step—a celebration of your contribution to the customer that culminates in a formal commitment. However, getting to this stage of your sales conversation and hammering the customer with a barrage of rebuttals and manipulation tactics does little more than push the customer away. In Australia and many Western cultures negotiating is frequently referred to as haggling.

Ex-pat Australian Morry Morgan is the co-founder of Clark Morgan, one of Asia's largest and most successful corporate training firms and *BOOM!*'s strategic partner in China. In his book entitled *Selling Big to China*, Morry delves into his 10-plus years of experience selling in China, the world's fastest growing market. He also provides insights into Asian business culture. What struck me most after reading Morry's book and then visiting China for the first time was how culturally contrasting Eastern and Western business cultures are when it comes to engaging in negotiation. For instance, in China, a discount is expected as part of the buying process. In Western culture asking for a discount is customarily met with an uncomfortable neck twitch and pursed lips, 'Hmmm, that's the best I can do, there's just no more room to move. Sorry.' In this situation a customer is often lost, not because their request for a discount wasn't met, but because there was no attempt to acknowledge the motive behind the request and to make the customer feel included in the buying process.

In China considerable importance is placed on fostering goodwill in negotiations, which derives from making a genuine attempt to negotiate a win–win outcome for both parties. In China your goodwill is vital in setting the foundations for long-term success and ongoing relationships and it is measured as such. The rule of make less now to gain more at a later date often applies.

Helping the other party to save face in negotiations is also fundamental in China, whereas in Western culture, few concessions are made in this area, because a winner takes all approach prevails. I have been on both sides of that equation, so I can attest that neither side of the fence is pleasant, particularly when you're being bent over it! In the West, we have a more short-term focus and limited insights into what constitutes effective negotiations. There is of course a more ruthless side to this ancient culture that I will explore with you in chapter 7. We have some catching up to do on our skills in these areas, particularly as our economy matures and becomes more engaged with the Asian markets.

If you know the enemy and know yourself you need not fear the results of a hundred battles.

Sun Tzu, ancient Chinese general and author of *The Art of War*

Buy the pants off them

Who do you think appeals to someone more—a person buying or a person selling something? Usually the buyer wins every time. The buyer contributes to the other person, whether by way of their success, credibility or financial gain. On every street corner we see brands on billboards adorned with colourful images and pithy strap lines. Turn on your TV and there are more ads selling you things you neither need nor want. Answer the phone and you hear a self-focused stranger trying to sell you something. In the heady pursuit of success, the fatal mistake many people make is that they sell and self-promote all the time, not leaving much opportunity for the customer to buy. Like spamming, this approach just trains people to ignore you.

Customers love buying, so don't ruin the experience for them: give your customers the opportunity to buy in before you rip into your sales spiel. Today, with more people than ever selling, the challenge for business is to come up with new, compelling ways to outsell their competition. But let me stop you right there: don't make the same mistakes your competitors make—instead create fresh and meaningful ways to deliver more!

As salespeople we get seduced and caught up in 'the sell' and getting what we want, but in doing so we can forget what it means to actually buy. In fact, the customer's buying experience takes a back seat to the salesperson's own needs. The result is that we then sell things we don't believe in to simply get paid. We remove all traces of our passion and conviction, and we aren't prepared to fight.

But customers aren't stupid: they can smell fear and this type of self-focused salesperson a mile off. So if you're leading with the sell, chances are you're finding things challenging and customers hard to come by.

One plus one equals three

One happy customer plus another should equal three. Clearly I failed mathematics at school, or is there more to it?

We all exist in a hyper-connected and transparent business world. If customers aren't sharing their positive experiences about you with others, something about what you do needs to change. Although competition is ferocious and margins are being eroded, customers still and always will pay for value and quality service. In fact, as customers, we crave it. Couple that with convenience and you have a strong value proposition.

The most ineffective businesses commonly lack repeat customers. These salespeople are unaccommodating and the engagement process is transactional at best. Conversely, more successful companies employ methods that ensure they obtain not only a customer's trust, but a commitment that inspires loyalty and repeat business. Despite what many people think, standing out in today's market isn't all that hard, given that the bar is set so low. Meaningful interactions are hard to find, and so the companies that are willing to provide genuine customer service are standing out. You can effectively differentiate by doing the simple things that matter most—these are not all that hard or expensive. Care about what you do and how you impact others. When you start caring and sharing value with customers you will find the market a lot more sympathetic to your demands.

When you stop seeing your customers as faceless numbers and start treating them as valuable assets over an extended period, they will see more value in you. This makes influencing and leading your customers to the benefits easier and more rewarding for all parties.

Learn your ABCs

Glengarry Glen Ross is an iconic movie starring Alec Baldwin, Al Pacino, Kevin Spacey and Jack Lemmon, among others. If you're in business and you haven't watched this movie yet, then go and hire it. It is about a team of desperate New York real estate agents who find themselves embroiled in a scandal (involving police) about one of the four salesman stealing the good leads from the manager's office: high-value prospect details printed on small cards. In one of the early scenes, Alec Baldwin's character, Blake, the obnoxious sales manager, unleashes a cantankerous, so-called pep-talk, containing a barrage of insults. In this scene he is sent by the owners of a real-estate sales office to improve the flagging efforts of the employees through threats, intimidation and the gimmick of a sales contest, in which first prize is a Cadillac, second prize, 'a set of steak knives', and third prize, 'you're fired'. Blake tells Lemmon's character, Shelley Levene, an ageing and struggling former sales star who gets up to refill his coffee mug, 'Coffee's for closers', implying Levene cannot have coffee, since he is not a closer. If you think your sales manager is a halfwit, you may see them in a better light after watching the sleazy Blake in action. You will also be clearer on the dark art of closing the sale and why this technique is seen as antiquated today.

Some salespeople (still) believe closing is the most important sales skill. Although closing, or the gain agreement phase of the ESP, is important, it's not the most important. Closing implies a level of control over a situation, a completion or finalisation of sorts. As a salesperson you never control anything: the best you will do is facilitate a process that moves the customer through the sales conversation—providing them with the right information to make the right decision.

If there is a close to be made, that right is reserved for the customer: only the customer can make that decision, making the close something you are best served avoiding. I can thank sleazy Blake for inspiring me with an idea that has become a big part of the success of my sales training programs. In the movie, mid rant, Blake moves to a whiteboard to elaborate the ABCs, which stands for Always Be Closing! Today, we all know closing is outdated, and that customers are too savvy to fall for primitive closing techniques, so the new ABCs as they relate to being an Outlaw are Always Be Contributing.

To achieve this you will need to stop closing and start contributing to the sales conversation and taking an interested in your customers' best interests. Look for new and interesting ways you can add value and enhance benefits for your customer. Deliver more. 'Sign here!' is a waste of time unless you're contributing first. Don't be like Blake: create a reputation for being a valuable contributor to your customers. Every day practise your ABCs.

When the time is right, ask for the business!

When my fiancée and I were building a new house for our ever-expanding family we met with Gary, who appeared to be an experienced sales consultant from one of our short-listed builders, in fact our preferred builder, to negotiate the final stages. What surprised me in this meeting was how little Gary tried to influence us in the final stage of the process.

Given Gary had done an adequate job up to this point over several meetings, and we were now ready to buy, this was the time he should have taken the bull by the horns and asked for the business as a logical next step. Instead he lacked confidence and when we quizzed him on a number of minor details, he retreated and seemed unsure of the answers. He then became defensive, which pushed us in the opposite direction. As a result my partner and I left this meeting confused and went to meet with option two, our next-preferred builder. When we walked through his door, he welcomed us like old family friends. After a number of meetings, armed with most of the hard work Gary had already done, we gleefully put pen to paper.

I'm all for taking a measured sales approach by developing the relationship first to create buy-in as you work to a tested process, but then when it comes time to ask for the business, don't hold back! Ask for the business with confidence and conviction!

Many salespeople, much like Gun Shy Gary, suffer from rejection anticipation because they are so accustomed to dealing with time-wasters and rejection—they start to expect it. This mindset then becomes a self-fulfilling prophecy, one that fuels under-achievement and diminishes credibility and results.

You need to lead your customers with confidence in the final stages of your process. If you have been working to a tested process like the ESP, your customer will expect it. Create a safe environment for them, take your time and remember to really listen to the conversation to pick up on subtle cues and clues to indicate when the customer is really ready to move and formalise a commitment. Have confidence in your ability to deliver more, and then just ask for the business!

My pistols, however, I always kept by me.

Jesse James, Outlaw

A winning attitude

The gain agreement phase is a real buzz! An agreement means a win, and all your time, skill and energy have been validated. Having a client invest substantial amounts of money in you, to trust you and buy what you sell, is not only healthy for your self-esteem, it should be your ultimate outcome. It's not uncommon for me to consult with a company and find many salespeople with 'loser' printed across their foreheads. I say that respectfully, of course. These people don't win new business often enough to be categorised as winners, some of them not making a sale for months on end. Why are they still employed?

Perhaps it's not all their own doing; maybe they don't have the right process, training or leadership. All these elements are fundamental to just about every sales team. In any case, you need to keep investing in your own training and development, so despite what's going on around you, you're still learning and growing forward.

Like passion, success is contagious and highly addictive. When you get on a roll, it feels like nothing can stop you! Meetings go from grey to black or white. Your customers believe and trust in you, and want to be led by you. You're now their trusted adviser; this is an honour and privilege. And, provided you don't get too full of yourself, this is a winning mindset—just let your competitors try to stop you.

Expect nothing less than to win. Don't take over-zealous risks, instead push yourself to deliver more. Customers want to buy from someone who is prepared to back themselves—a winner—so don't let them down.

> *You were born to win, but to be a winner, you must plan to win, prepare to win, and expect to win.*
>
> Zig Ziglar, author and motivational speaker

Can we always trust others to keep their word?

The following story highlights how more experienced salespeople don't even need to ask for the business, they apply a more subtle yet assertive approach.

Nigel dropped off his business suit for some alternations. The tailor greeted him with open arms. After some banter he suggested Nigel try on a new suit. It was smart, but Nigel said, 'Thanks anyway. Maybe next time.' Not willing to concede the tailor replied, 'Just let me size you up. If you like it, you can pick it up next week and just pay me whenever you can. I trust you.' Nigel resisted again, but the artful tailor continued to insist until Nigel capitulated. Later he asked the tailor if he did this for everyone, 'No, only for special clients.' Nigel took that as a compliment, though he suspected this was the tailor's standard process once he got to know someone.

Unlike the tailor, I believe in getting business agreements signed on the dotted line. I'm not legally qualified, but I've been privy to many verbal agreements being manipulated after the fact, leaving one or both parties at a disadvantage. There's an old saying that a contract isn't worth the paper it's written on. While this can be true at times, contracts do effectively bind people morally to an agreement, which tends to foster consistent behaviour, irrespective of legal obligations and ramifications.

The artful tailor understood and applied what best-selling author and persuasion expert Dr Robert Cialdini refers to as the Consistency Principle. By declaring his trust in Nigel, the artful tailor bound him to a perceived moral obligation and thus encouraged Nigel's behaviour to be consistent with the tailor's expectation.

The Consistency Principle correlates with the Pygmalion effect by suggesting that the greater the expectation placed upon people, often children or students and employees, the better they perform. The opposite also applies when your expectations are low. For example, if you overstate your legal position in the gaining agreement phase of the sale, this can spook your customer, as it suggests a lack of trust or it may be misinterpreted as aggression, encouraging the other party to be consistent with your position and mirror it back. But a complete disregard for legal rigor at this stage of the process is a sign of inexperience. Often salespeople skim over the small print in contracts in order to get the pen on the paper.

Back when I was a salivating desperado salesperson I would encourage this approach, but today I'm quick to point out any areas of contention in advance and to slow down the process if I need to. This not only builds trust, it safeguards against problems downstream. Although the effect of consistency on others is important, when financial wellbeing is at risk, people can and often do demonstrate unpredictable behaviour. The bottom line is that if the relationship is worth saving, it's worth signing.

How to apply positive tension

Influencing with a difference can be a challenge to assert from a distance. When you're not in front of your customers in some form, its more than likely you are failing to be even remotely part of their reality. Sure you really know your stuff, but that matters little to a customer who, in their own world, is just as busy as you are. Forget sitting in front of the phone or refreshing your inbox every 30 seconds. I'm sorry to be the bearer of bad news, but the customer is just not that into you.

Three types of tension

The vast majority of sales professionals apply no tension. This type of tension is passive. It requires no process or genuine short- or long-term interest in pursuing the customer to make the sale. As soon as the customer leaves the conversation they're swiftly removed from the salesperson's memory. If you don't create tension, it tells the customer you couldn't care less about them.

The second form of tension is called negative tension and it is a more aggressive form of connection. It can be used to jolt the customer into action and is commonly practised by arrogant salespeople who don't recognise the line between persistence and harassment. These tactics are based on pressure and manipulation and they can work, but they usually lead to buyer's remorse and remove any hope of goodwill, repeat business and referrals.

Positive tension is just that. It's a conscious connection between customer and salesperson. Both know where they stand, and a logical process is being followed and agreed at each step. Contact is initiated equally and return calls are made promptly. Mutual respect is felt, and accountabilities met. Sound like a sales nirvana? It doesn't have to be if you're having the right sales conversation. As in any successful relationship, the quality of your conversations is the key. When you're leaving messages after emails without reply, your customer is hearing you, but definitely not feeling you.

If you don't have a desire to chase up genuine client opportunities, or customers aren't coming back to you, you're in a negative tension, or no tension, zone. Should this be the case, check your mindset and tweak your approach. Negative-tension profiles require a complete strategy rethink. What is it about your offer and approach that is contributing and encouraging this type of negative tension state? Once identified, you need to move quickly to change your approach and prevent recurrences.

Positive-tension customers should be acknowledged and moved forward promptly. Remember that just because a potential high-value customer is always willing to give you their time, it doesn't guarantee their value. Are they initiating contact with you, or are you always contacting them? This can be a telling sign and give you a clearer sense of their interest. To create positive tension, try applying an educative approach to selling and work hard to always be contributing. Remember, if you're not contributing, you're either doing nothing or you are taking. Simply following up and touching base does little more than train your customers to ignore you.

Apply the Red Phone technique when following up and lead with insights or information that creates leverage. This could mean communicating new industry insights, the latest competitive advantage or technology, or something only you know, and they don't, about their competitors. Genuine positive tension is a powerful technique you can add to your tool belt to help you influence with a difference.

Understand the three levels of tension and play them to your advantage. Maintain the positive tension and your customer connections will be vastly more meaningful and valuable. Think about your current high-value clients and classify them according to one of the three tensions. This provides a guide for what type of tension you need to apply to replicate that type of customer in future.

> *The fibres of all things have their tension and are strained like the strings of an instrument.*
>
> Henry David Thoreau, author, poet and philosopher

The Pied Piper: Guy Gabaldon

One of the most impressive examples of influencing with a difference is the extraordinary story of a US marine in the Second World War. Guy Gabaldon had left his own family as a teenager, and moved in with a Japanese–American family. He attended language school every day with their children and learned to speak Japanese. After the Japanese attack on Pearl Harbor, his 'adopted' family, were sent to a relocation camp in Arizona and in 1943, on his seventeenth birthday, Gabaldon joined the US Marine Corps.

On the very first day the Marines arrived on Saipan, a Pacific island still held by the Japanese, Gabaldon began bringing in prisoners. The first night he went out on his own and brought back two prisoners using backstreet Japanese to persuade them to surrender. He was reprimanded by his superior officers and threatened with a court-martial for leaving his post, but the next night he again defied the rules and the next morning he returned with 50 Japanese prisoners. As a result, Gabaldon was permitted by his commanding officer to act as a lone wolf. Around 1500 soldiers and civilians surrendered to Gabaldon and were turned over to the United States military authorities. For his exploits, Gabaldon became known as the Pied Piper of Saipan.

How did he achieve this level or influence with enemy soldiers? It all started with a single piece of critical information that Gabaldon communicated in Japanese to the enemy. He searched at night and found one enemy soldier and told them that the location the Japanese soldiers occupied was going to be bombed. He then offered a deal: if the soldiers surrendered to him he would guarantee their safety, shelter and food. For the cold, hungry Japanese soldiers hiding in the hills this was alluring, but most critically, he gave them the choice to save their own lives. This is the Red Phone principle in action. His critical information, and the fearless way in which he delivered it, influenced enemy soldiers to agree with his terms. Gabaldon then marched them back unarmed into the US prison camp, not just once, but night after night. Gabaldon's story also highlights the power of process—when you get the process right, it allows you to replicate the outcome time and again.

Imagine what you could achieve if you applied even a fraction of Gabaldon's courage and determination to the way you sell? Gabaldon was like any salesperson: though his circumstances were extraordinary, his success relied solely on his ability to influence with a difference and help the enemy solider to see the situation through his eyes. Ultimately he influenced his enemy with empathy. His upbringing helped, of course, illustrating the vital importance of having a commonality in sales, as it breaks down barriers quickly and helps to build trust. Equally important, the Pied Piper genuinely cared about saving the lives of the Japanese, but he also achieved this in a way that served the US Marines: a true win–win outcome.

Gabaldon defied the rules and risked punishment but his results were so staggering, his superiors could not deny him permission to carry out his self-imposed missions. This is how he drove change and set new precedents for others to follow.

Results will always speak louder than words: when your results are significant enough, they scream to those that need to hear it! If your aim is to influence your manager, get the results first, because this gives you leverage to negotiate. If you want to influence customers, again leverage is key — this is where critical information comes in. You will also need to lead with results through past experiences coupled with your ability to tell your story in a compelling way. Take the customer to a place where they can see, feel and taste the value, and then keep leading them to the benefits. Gabaldon also delivered by coming back with more prisoners night after night. Not surprisingly, when you deliver more, you will always achieve more.

☞ Action points ☜

- Know your ABCs: Always Be Contributing. Develop a reputation as a salesperson who works hard to deliver more value for customers.

- Apply a winning mindset. If you expect to win, this changes your approach. If you want to be a winner, act like one.

- Apply positive tension and your customer connections will not only be more positive, they will also be more valuable.

- The gain agreement stage of the sales process shouldn't be tense and stressful. If you don't enjoy the process, the customer won't either.

- Gaining agreement is a celebration of commitment, so enjoy it and party hard!

CHAPTER 7

FIGHT 'TIL THE END

The ultimate measure of a man is not where he stands in moments of comfort and convenience, but where he stands at times of challenge and controversy.

Martin Luther King, Jr, civil rights leader

Persistence and resilience are the measure of a person who is truly committed to their cause. Sales professionals are expected to compete 48 weeks or more every year. It's no wonder most are burnt out and exhausted. Nearly all performance activities are structured in a way so the performer competes for a small fraction of their time in comparison with the amount of time spent refining their skills and training, and developing strategy, as well as in recovery. Sales managers, for their own and sometimes bizarre reasons, believe that their salespeople don't need the same approach. This belief limits their team's success and ultimately leads to fatigue, apathy and burnout, sending even the most committed of individuals to a place where they start questioning their abilities and actions.

How to overcome fatigue, apathy and burnout

To play the A-game, you will need to be fresh in mind, body and spirit. When you are tired and under strain, not only does your performance suffer, but the passion and pleasure associated with what you do also diminishes—rapidly. I habitually ask salespeople that I sense have low motivation levels whether, if they were succeeding more, they would be more motivated. The overwhelming response is always an enthusiastic 'Yes!' When salespeople are low in energy their performance suffers, and so does their job satisfaction. It's not that they don't enjoy their role, rather that the role isn't providing them with the required validation and reward for effort. Salespeople are more effective when they are focused, energised and working towards clear goals in a structured approach.

A business can survive without many things, but its commercial life is severely limited without sales. As a sales leader, give your salespeople the support they need with habitual training and development, a clearly defined process and relevant tools, and of course inspiring leadership. Salespeople rarely leave a company: they leave a manager, making the leadership and culture vital in developing team members over an extended period. Sales professionals need to be in their role for at least 12 months to gain any real traction. The longer the right salespeople are in the role, the more confident and skilled they become. Experience speaks volumes. The most successful teams hang onto their high performers over an extended period. In contrast, less successful teams churn through talented team members and do little more than train their competitors and surrender valuable intellectual property.

I also encourage HiPer-salespeople to take breaks periodically so they can reflect on their strategy. They may not want to take a break, but it's in their best interest and the company's that they take some time out to re-energise and quieten the mind. This will lead to more energy, improved job satisfaction and enhanced performance.

Belief is not important: it's everything

Many capable people begin doubting themselves when they are put under pressure, and so they retract instead of forging ahead with confidence. Stress affects people in different ways. Some thrive and it enhances their focus, while others regress into trembling fools incapable of executing even the simplest fundamentals.

If you're in the game, you're good enough to win it! When it comes to competitors, never doubt yourself under pressure against a more successful rival. They have more to lose than you. Ignore the whispers of uncertainty. Demand excellence and when opportunity knocks, seize the moment. The cost of not doing so is years of regret—some people never get over those missed opportunities, the regret festering as they play the scenario over and over again in their heads. Every year monumental upsets are achieved in business. The most memorable victories are nearly always achieved by the underdog who truly believes they can win, not just by applying their skills but also through sheer will. The underdog's best friend is called Belief—she's an inspiring co-pilot, so never doubt her wisdom.

Save you? Save me!

Okay, so you've taken on a new salesperson or sales target and things aren't quite going to plan; business is slow and customers are cautious. Unperturbed, you push forward, hammering away with greater intensity, hoping this will move you faster towards your goal. You have a few small wins here and there, but not enough to get your sales manager off your back. He is demanding and now he's really riding you hard. You review your level of passion on the passion-meter: it's down two points since your last assessment, now at five out of 10. You're on the edge, so you consult with a trusted adviser, who has a way of helping you see your challenges differently and energising you. The pep talk serves you well—after another two weeks you finally have another win. Validation! Things are now looking up, taking your spirit with them.

Three more weeks pass, another lag. Your passion is depleted, and so is your morale. Your manager's spitting venom at you, demanding results! You are feeling the pressure externally and internally. 'This is crazy!' you think. You start questioning yourself. Consumed with thoughts like, maybe this industry is not for me? I just don't think I'm cut out for this type of selling. You start cursing all the time-wasters who ignore your emails and follow-up calls.

You again look externally for more assistance. You start speaking with friends and colleagues about your situation; everyone feels sympathy for you but no-one can help you. You feel trapped, and your back is to the wall.

Here's where we hit the pause button!

This is the stage where most people give up. They formally tender their resignation or they surrender mentally. The pressure is so intense, the most logical response appears to be flight. But as an Outlaw this is your moment to dig in and fight. To meet the challenge, and show who you really are and that your determination is stronger than the challenge. Get angry if you need to, but make sure you channel your anger into action.

Giving up at the critical stage will always limit your potential. It weakens your personal resilience and enhances your reliance on others; this state of need then transmutes into a hazardous mindset that teaches you to lean on others when times are tough.

If you're struggling and finding the challenge overwhelming, turning to trusted advisers is your first option. Put your ego aside, and be brutally honest and vulnerable. It's essential you get candid advice here to assess your options. A word of caution: when you pay for this type of advice you can often meet people who are pushing their own agendas. At this stage of the game, trusting your intuition or making the hardest decision can be your smartest option. Unbiased advice is really important.

The best mentors I know don't need to charge a fee: they simply get a buzz from helping like-minded people. You must know someone who is successful or has impressive credentials, and a request to bend their ear will rarely meet with disapproval. Just be sure you're seeking wisdom rather a desperate plea for help or money—this is a turn-off for anyone.

The easiest decision is always to quit, and this makes absolute sense if you genuinely lack a passion for what you're doing. If the passion is concealed underneath a lack of results, it's time to refine your strategy and get back to basics.

It's not that I'm so smart, it's just that I stay with problems longer.

Albert Einstein, physicist

If you're running your own business, this stage may force you to consider bringing in a partner to help carry the load. Proceed here with caution. To succeed, the commercial fits must be logical and allow each party to contribute uniquely. Also consider who is *really* saving whom in the relationship? Or do both parties need to be saved? Overlook these critical pieces of insight and you will all go down with the ship. Business partners will come and go. Paid mentors will eventually move on. Money will be raised and then churned through. Targets will be missed and then reset. The bar will always rise. If you set a target, make sure you have the energy and motivation to see it through. There will always be challenges — usually more than you have planned for, so plan for success. Before you consider getting someone to save you, invest more in the development of your own skills and be willing to really push through. The best person to save you is always you.

When yes means no and red means go

As customers, we have all walked into a retail environment with our arms crossed and absolutely no intention of buying. We then trot out 20 minutes later with our bags loaded, scratching our head but feeling strangely pleased with ourselves. Conversely, think of a customer that enters a used car lot with a wide smile and wallet visibly open. Yet, they spend two hours labouring over the purchase and then walk out with nothing but an insincere, 'I'll need to sleep on it, but I'll be back tomorrow I promise.'

These cues and buying signals can wreak havoc on a salesperson's confidence, leaving them unclear, reactive and untrusting of their own instincts. Outlaws don't just trust their instincts: they work to a tested process. They understand when yes really means no, so they're rarely caught off guard and their time is utilised effectively. They really listen in order to pick up on subtle cues like body language and tone to help them get a clearer sense of what is truly being said. They also know from past experience what success looks like, so they move the sales conversation towards the various scenarios that need to play out to create the desired outcomes.

When most salespeople see a red light and feel the overwhelming urge to stop, Outlaws keep going, adapting and drilling deeper. A red light is seen as a moment to pause, refine and advance with enhanced clarity. This elevates them above other salespeople. A customer who fails to return your calls isn't necessarily avoiding you on purpose: it could mean they're genuinely busy in their own world. You may be important, but not before more pressing matters. Misreading the signals here could translate into your disregarding a genuine customer or mutating into a salivating carpark stalker and pushing them away. When you see the signals for what they really are, you can press forward or change course with confidence. The words maybe or no are then seen merely as a red light waiting to turn green.

Sheer persistence can overcome brilliance

'Twelve hundred dollar!' snapped Lily. 'No way, too much,' I snorted. The pocket-rocket snatched the calculator from me and punched in a counter-offer: 'One thousand!' 'No, no. Still too expensive,' I replied. Back and forth went the calculator like a tennis ball fizzing over the net in a grand slam final. Deep into the fifth set, Lily's frustration became obvious, her wide smile morphing to a frown. I had moved in the negotiations marginally, while she had discounted to less than 10 per cent of her initial asking price. But that's how the game is played in downtown Shanghai, China — a bustling marketplace replete with all the delights and junk a discount-hungry tourist can buy.

Lily and I ground to an agreement. She sneered, 'You a tough man.' With a chuckle, I said 'zài jiàn' knowing I had still left money on the table. But, to spend another five minutes squabbling over what was essentially a few dollars seemed counterproductive. It was my last day in China and I was on a mission to buy as much cheap stuff as I could in the smallest amount of time. In every stall I observed salespeople applying a similar method. They always request a ridiculously high price. Rejected by the customer, the salesperson asks what the customer wants to spend. Incremental counter-offers then move the customer towards a price that both agree on. In the West, haggling is frowned on; in Asia, it's simply part of a common respected and tested sales process.

If you look more closely at this technique, you will find some real genius. For one, the salespeople apply their process and fully trust in it, and it rarely fails them. They begin by asking what the customer wants to pay, successfully gauging the customer's expectations. They proceed to explain all the benefits of the product to position it in its most valuable light. The salesperson then sets a price; the customer's counter-offer establishes their level of buy-in. And so the process moves forward.

The salesperson understands that the more time a customer spends in dialogue with them, the more likely they are to buy. If a considerable amount of time passes in negotiations, and the customer then walks, I have witnessed amiable vendors mutating into spitting vipers — disgusted by the customer exiting the sales conversation without an outcome. In short, they are fiercely conscious of their time and how important every opportunity is. Wasted time is dead money.

Most importantly, they demonstrate the most vital element of success in any field: persistence. Incredibly relentless in their pursuit of the sale, these salespeople work with a tested method that most Western salespeople couldn't be bothered with. This process is gruelling, with every target customer being engaged in a structured and patient way, and it takes discipline, persistence and resilience — essential characteristics for success, no matter where in the world you do business.

Persistence is to the character of man as carbon is to steel.

Napoleon Hill, author of *Think and Grow Rich*

Crack the whip!

When is the worst time to get urgent? When you really need to! When client proposals are sitting on desks for weeks or clients are waiting too long for a response, you can be sure your business is suffering. Remember the curse of complacency: just like passion, it's also highly contagious. In low-performing sales teams you will see team members merely going through the motions with no accountability or consequences for a lack of results. There is little pride in what they do and few are prepared to fight for what they believe in.

Someone in your company needs to be the panic merchant. This person shouldn't always be the CFO—though most are adept in the dark arts of panic, seeing the business through the prism of numbers. You have got to get urgent *now* for your own success. Countless businesses underperform because no-one in the organisation has a sufficient sense of urgency, or not enough people in the team are urgent.

Be the cause, not the sum, of things that affect you. Each day you get up, you may be weary, but you always need to be hungry. Drive your business irrespective of targets and bonuses. Do it because you want to, not because you have to. It's better to get urgent now, rather than later when you might really need to. Proactive urgency is powerful, whereas reactive urgency often defaults to desperation, and no-one likes a desperado.

Know your magic numbers

People who disregard a tested process will skip vital steps and go for the customer's jugular every time. Sure they may get a quick win here and there, but more often than not a tested and measurable approach is more effective. My father is an enthusiastic recreational fisherman and he taught me everything I know about fishing. As a youngster, one of my first lessons was to always keep the line tight. That means when you hook a fish, don't give it any slack line to throw the hook. In sales, the same principle applies to communication. Don't give a genuine customer an excuse to go cold or lose interest: keep the lines of communication tight, apply positive tension and ensure you are following up methodically and leading the your customer at every stage of your process.

Here are some metrics on outbound calls to sales prospects. While you should keep in mind that there are exceptions to every rule, these statistics are powerful:

- **1 per cent** of sales are made on the first contact.

- **2 per cent** of sales are made on the second contact.

- **5 per cent** of sales are made on the third contact.

- **12 per cent** of sales are made on the fourth contact.

- **80 per cent** of sales are made on the fifth (or later) contact.

Most salespeople surrender after the second or third attempt at contact. You can see from the list above how that approach limits their results. But also make sure you don't make contact for the sake of making contact—that's called harassment. One of the most effective methods to help you understand how many contacts you should make is to measure your data. This data should reveal some magic numbers. How many contacts on average do you conduct to make a sale? What is the best-case contact scenario for you? What is the worst case? Which metrics translated into happy and profitable customers? Which created dissatisfied ones?

To the fighting man, peace is sure.

Irish Proverb

Don't fail to follow up

Following up is one of the most underrated and under-utilised skills in business. Following up is nothing more than communication: it's positive tension that demonstrates professionalism and that you genuinely care about and value your customer. Following up isn't calling or emailing periodically and asking for a decision, nor is it simply calling to say hi, without any new critical information. Following up means developing a consistent method to lead your customer through each stage of your process. In this process, over time, you will get to understand the magic numbers that are working for you that will provide you with a guide to measure how many times you should be following up and at what frequency.

When your follow-up process starts to exceed your magic number, for example, your magic number is five and you are now at the tenth follow-up call and your communication is now defined as negative or no tension, you should change your approach drastically. Ideally, your follow-up method should be stated in your initial conversations with the customer, particularly when you're talking about time frames for delivery of information required in your pre-sales. This sets the tone for positive tension, safeguards you both from feeling uncomfortable when you initiate follow-up and ensures that expectations for ongoing communication are aligned.

Remember, there is a fine line between persistence and harassment, so set a verbal agenda by letting the client know the motive behind your follow-up process and how it benefits them. Equally, asking for permission to follow up can also provide your customer with a sense of ease and buy-in, so they feel you are not ambushing them at inopportune times. Following up effectively isn't hard, but it does require an understanding of your magic numbers, positive tension, discipline and time—all best utilised in a structured approach. When you take following up seriously, serious results will follow.

Find the contrast

In Viktor Frankl's disturbing yet fascinating work *Man's Search for Meaning*, he tells of his harrowing experiences as a prisoner in a Nazi concentration camp. One of the methods he and the other prisoners used for survival was to fantasise about things they enjoyed back in the real world, such as eating their favourite foods, while they starved or gagged as they ate muck not fit for animals. Many prisoners who survived torture or escaped death would eventually go insane. Frankl and others, despite their environment, chose to see their reality differently, and as a result kept their sanity intact. Frankl's personal story is one of tremendous adversity, yet in our world many people are easily seduced into apathy from experiences that pale into significance. Your stresses are, of course, very real to you, but to someone else they are insignificant.

You can choose to see your current situation differently or you can change your current situation by doing something completely different. Drive change! Just remember, when you start relying on external forces for motivation and validation, you are by default choosing to let someone else determine your self-worth. As an Outlaw you are externally focused but internally driven. The space between thinking and action is consciousness. When you are aware and alert to how your thoughts play out in the real world, you will guard them with your life. Only you can determine how you feel and you have the grit and determination to see your vision come true.

Embrace the struggle

Can you imagine peeling open your sleepy eyes in the morning, staring vaguely up at the ceiling, and believing you have nothing to live for? The concept of life having no meaning is enough to terrify even the most optimistic of people into unrelenting depression. It's much easier to quickly jump into the shower, throw on some clothes, down a quick stiff coffee and strategically position ourselves in the morning traffic. It's best not to think about such things too much—it only triggers confusion and de-motivation.

Meaningful relationships, meaningful conversations and meaningful careers are just a few of the many ways we seek out meaning in a cold and confusing world. Fail to find meaning and you lose purpose followed by passion and without passion, success is difficult to realise because you won't have the determination to push through challenges.

Irrespective of our flaws and misgivings, humans are without question more intellectually advanced than ever before, thanks to the information and media explosion over the last few decades. With more information this makes us more cunning and also more open to exploring mutually beneficial outcomes. We are not longer as willing to be led down the garden path blindly, never questioning things that don't feel right—this in itself is one of humanity's greatest achievements.

This is a monumental opportunity for us. If it feels wrong to you, explore what is not suggested and have your own opinions and draw your own conclusions. Why do we let a small minority control and influence the majority with fear and aggression? Why do we need to keep ourselves busy, even to the detriment of our health and those we love? Why are we so fearful of failure and what others think?

How would you re-live your life knowing what you know now? Would you:

- take more risks?

- follow your passion?

- spend more time with your loved ones?

- fear failure?

- work less and play more?

- be more romantic, more loving?

- be honest, even if it hurts you?

- face up to that bully and fight?

This is your moment—seize it. This is your world—embrace it. This is your time—enjoy it. Life is not a rehearsal, so act. Don't pretend you know all the answers, because you don't. Just get on with life and make the most of it.

> *Live as if you were living a second time, and as though you had acted wrongly the first time.*
>
> Viktor Frankl, Holocaust survivor, neurologist and psychiatrist

Every so often it feels like the universe is conspiring against us. No matter how vigorously we toil nothing seems to go our way. Done deals fall over at the eleventh hour. Hot prospects inexplicably vanish into vapour. People who owe us money go on holiday. It seems the only people willing to speak to us are trying to sell *us* something! Although this seemingly negative force is raging now, it will eventually cease and swiftly flow in the opposite direction. Similarly, all money markets spiral down, correct, and then shoot to the sky yet again. Record sales periods morph into slumps, sometimes for no clear reason. Keeping your head up and your motivation levels high help you survive challenging times.

When times are tough learn to ride them out. The tide will turn: it's just a matter of time. It's never easy, but don't let short-term obstacles and challenges consume you. You can question things at times, that's logical, but don't fixate on them for too long. Change your approach and tweak your strategy, but don't give up: the tide will turn. Remember our potential is found just beyond our breaking point. We habitually surrender at the identical stage of a journey each time: this position is our pain threshold, and it can be predicted with accuracy. Interestingly, it's that point that determines our growth and ultimate success, so know where your pain threshold is and do your best to smash through it.

You will break through eventually. If you don't believe in yourself, how can you expect others to? Failure builds character and resilience. Failure reveals insights to advance your skills. Failure is beautiful, if you dare to look inside. When you overcome failure it not only boosts your confidence, it's exhilarating.

The big stick

A few days after New Year's Day, Stella went to the gym, armed with her new year's resolution. She drove into the car park, but struggled to find even one vacant spot. In a huff, she exited the gym car park and reluctantly parked two blocks up the street, and walked back to the gym. When she entered the front door, she noticed the gym was packed full of sweaty bodies puffing, pulling and straining. Stella took a tour of the gym with the manager. At the end of the tour, the manager took Stella through the prices and membership options. Stella was happy with the club and amenities, but she had one overwhelming concern. She turned to the gym manager and asked if the gym was always this busy — having to line up and wait to use the equipment was a big concern for her. The manager chuckled and responded in an ironic tone, 'Don't worry, Stella. In a few weeks, the gym will be half empty. Just you wait and see.'

Hence the lesson: most people who declare a new year's resolution aren't prepared to stick at it long enough to see their goal achieved. The resolution is a token gesture, born more from other people's expectations instead of coming from a place of true meaning and purpose. Everyone needs a new year's resolution, right? One or two weeks and maybe a setback or two and they quit the goal, resigned to the murky backwaters of procrastination once again. It's common knowledge that gyms make most of their money from members not showing up. Anyone can set a goal, but only the persistent and resilient few have the discipline to see it through. The best way to achieve goals is to set small and realistic goals and then truly commit to seeing them through. This builds confidence to enable you to then increase the size and importance of your goals accordingly.

Don't set a goal unless it's truly important to you. Then declare it to the world and fight for it.

I am extraordinarily patient, provided I get my own way in the end.

Margaret Thatcher, longest serving Prime Minister of the United Kingdom

Where success and defeat meet

A photo finish decided the 2011 Melbourne Cup, the world's richest horse race. Only the benefit of cutting-edge photo-technology could confirm the faintest spectre of light between first and second place. The winner, Dunaden, pocketed $3.6 million in prize money—as for the horse that ran second, its name had already escaped me just moments after the race.

Even though you are fighting for a meaningful goal, the difference between being remembered and not being recalled at all can be minuscule. Frequently, contracts are won on minor details, not necessarily major points of difference. Failure can be measured in millimetres. It's these crushing blows to our confidence and self-esteem that either spur us on to bolder heights, or corral us in defeat. If you have lost a pitch or a project you were desperate to win, it's what you do next that best defines you.

Next time you taste defeat take some time to reflect. Did you really give it your all? If not, what areas can you improve on next time? If you are competing against a worthy foe, perhaps there are some things they do that you can integrate into your offer or approach. If you surrender to defeat, you will never grow or improve, and it's the pain and lessons from your most monumental losses that become your best assets. Much like the Melbourne Cup, success is a race for stayers. Sprinters don't qualify. To win you need strength, endurance and most importantly the will to succeed. It doesn't matter where you are placed on the final turn, it's how you finish that matters most — how you finish is how you will be remembered.

Navigating by a lone star

Can you be a star twinkling high above everyone else, every day? More realistically, you could be shining only some of the time. You will have ups and downs — perhaps a good part of your career will be defined by downs. For an Outlaw, it is not how many times you succeed, but how many times you fail, get back up, dust yourself off and get back on the horse again.

- How much rejection are you willing to endure?

- How much instant gratification can you forgo?

- How many nos will you hear and stay on track and focused?

- How many naysayers will you dismiss?

Anyone can thrive in a bull market — true success is sticking to it through the tough times.

The thing to understand about Outlaws is that they don't try to shine, but like the Chens and Pied Pipers of this world, over time, they just do. Who they are shines bright and resonates, touching people's lives and contributing lasting value. Selling is nothing more than leading customers to a win–win outcome. Sell something you believe in with such conviction that the simple act of speaking about it to others turns them on, too.

The game changer

In Malcolm Gladwell's insightful book *Outliers: The Story of Success*, he reveals after extensively researching high-performance people from various disciplines and walks of life that it takes roughly 10 000 hours of practice to achieve mastery in any field. That's more than 10 years of relevant, focused practice. If you are practising in the wrong way, of course, you will need to wait considerably longer before you can claim mastery. How many people ever stick at something that long? It's so easy to jump when things are not going to plan, but in doing so we remove any likelihood of really growing in confidence and capability. The key to mastery is to keep learning and keep growing.

And a true master knows there is no such thing as mastery.

When you believe you have nothing left to give, this is usually a sign you are closer than you think. Similarly, when you think have nothing left to learn, life will usually find a way of proving otherwise. A pledge to learn and grow, even if those around you are not as committed to this process, is a profound way of being. One of the best ways to learn more about yourself is to simply ask the people around you who know you best, your trusted advisers. In their eyes, what are your strengths and areas for development? Maybe some of your customers have valuable insights you can apply, too? One thing is for sure: your clients won't mind giving you constructive feedback because your request usually demonstrates an interest in being a better person or in better serving them in some way.

One of the great things about trying new things and being open to learning is that you never know where it may lead you. You may buy a book or attend a seminar and receive little lasting value. You may walk in with empty pockets and leave with a sack full of gold. My experience at a training program many years ago was spectacularly golden. During the course of this program I was led to a rare 'Aha!' moment.

One that jolted me with so much clarity I saw the world differently.

Here's that thought: 'How can I ever be complacent or bored in my chosen profession, if I'm constantly striving to improve?' With that small thought, my game changed.

Consider a successful musician spending their lifetime in search of the perfect ballad or stage performance? A politician who climbs the ranks in Parliament with a single-minded focus to change the world without compromising her values? Think of an athlete striving for their personal best, rising before dawn, year in year out, sacrificing their personal life in the pursuit of being better. Surely they must get complacent doing the same thing tirelessly, over and over again? But champions never do, because they are invigorated by the journey and the pursuit of excellence.

Finally we shall place the Sun himself at the centre of the Universe.

Nicolaus Copernicus, astronomer

Outlaws commit to an outward progression in the pursuit of contributing to their customers and the industries they work in. Outlaws never follow the tired standards of others: instead they blaze a meaningful path that illuminates others. This journey is fraught with danger yet tantalisingly laced with adventure. They drive change to establish a fresh way of seeing and navigating the world that inspires others. They commit to a body of work that can span a decade or a lifetime, a life they can be proud of.

When you harness the Outlaw spirit, you will meet challenges and setbacks head on, but these are only tests to determine whether you are truly prepared to fight for what you believe in. An Outlaw's ultimate destiny is never about riches or fame: it's always about changing the game—the rules of the game start and end with you.

☞ **Action points** ☜

- Believe in yourself or no-one else will.

- Sheer persistence will overcome brilliance. Know your magic numbers and don't fail to follow up.

- If you really want it, fight to the death!

- Stay hungry. Get urgent now before you really need to.

- Education is your most powerful weapon. Use it to empower yourself and others. Keep learning and keep growing.

Conclusion

Outlaw principles to sell and live by

As an Outlaw you have, not a right, but an undeniable opportunity to follow a career you can be endlessly enthused by. When it's all said and done, you can hang your worn hat on a way of doing business you can be proud of. This path is rarely the road most travelled: instead it's a choice and a direction in life that will lead you on a more meaningful and purposeful journey. Outlaws are seldom reckless: they are calculated and cunning in realising what they set out to achieve.

We live in a world of ceaseless movement, a world, by and large, defined by change and progress, so why not be the driver and determine your own destiny? When you drive change and commit to this process from a place of deep knowing you harness a primal urge that dwells in all of us — to contribute to others and leave a lasting legacy. Just let the naysayers try to deny you when you are this fiercely committed to your cause.

To influence and make a difference you must always aim to deliver more. In fact, the best measure of an Outlaw is this ability, along with your customer's willingness to be led by you through uncertainty. As time passes, many things around you will change — technology, the company you keep, and of course some of your ambitions — but what won't change are your intrinsic values. These are ever-lasting and unbreakable values that determine what you believe, and how you think and interact with others including your customers.

Equally steadfast are the seven Outlaw principles: you may question them from time to time and test them, but they will never fail you. They are built to endure the howling winds of change—all seven carefully constructed to help you make your mark and achieve your goals. Trust in them; guard them; and only share them with people you know that are equally committed to fighting for their customers and selling without fear.

1   *Dare to prepare.* Outlaws don't possess endless budgets: they are forced to innovate, invent and try new things. They don't just harness change—*they drive it!* Your default setting is to under-prepare, but demonstrating how much time and thought you are prepared to invest into each opportunity helps you to gain an edge over your competitors. Dare to prepare!

2   *Inspire with words and actions.* The Outlaw spirit is especially inspired when you transform key business functions and accelerate growth to create additional revenue streams and profit pathways. Buy in before you sell in. Your actions must always align with and reinforce your words. Be a rebel with a cause.

3   *Create a cult with personality.* To succeed in sales, I think you have to be a little nuts and able to see the world differently. As brazen and disruptive as Outlaws can be at times, they are equally conscious of how they impact others. Being true to yourself and taking a genuine interest in your customers makes you more interesting and engaging. Wave the pirate flag and deliver more!

4   *Harness the power of process.* An Outlaw is a trusted ally and a person of influence that customers call on for critical advice to *lead* them through challenges and uncertainty. Process is the mother of replication, so use your ESP to

guide your customers to the win–win outcome time and again. Always work to your tested process, but allow for some flexibility.

5 *Ignite the passion contagion.* Only sell a product you are genuinely passionate about. Be passionate about contributing to others. Be passionate about being the best you can be. Passion is highly contagious! But remember to tame your passion or you will meet Reckless.

6 *Influence with a difference.* Outlaws are prepared to fight for their customers and *deliver more!* More choice, more service and more value! This is the time to celebrate your commitment. This will mean defying the rules and doing what your competitors aren't prepared to do.

7 *Fight 'til the end.* Challenges are merely opportunities in disguise. Remember, if you're in the game you're good enough to win it. Outlaws understand that being chased by the popular opinion and flying in the face of industry standards comes with the territory and is indeed part of the thrill.

Apply each of the Outlaw principles in isolation and you will be more successful; however, when you harness all seven principles you will transform yourself from a mere salesperson into a genuine person of influence.

Fight for your customers and they will fight for you.

Index

Index

OUTLAW

The Outlaw selling program empowers you with the attributes and skills to be armed and dangerous, Most Wanted by your competitors, peers and, most importantly, by your customers.

After this revolutionary sales program you will:

✓ develop strategies to *defy the rules* and gain a distinct competitive advantage

✓ apply new skills to *drive change* and be a world-class communicator

✓ have the confidence and charisma to create a cult-like following

✓ harness the power of process to replicate success time and again

✓ ignite passion within yourself, your team and your customers

✓ be known as a real person of influence that *delivers more!*

✓ push through emotional road blocks to achieve your goals.

Who should attend?

Whether you're new to selling, a dogged veteran, a manager leading a team, an entrepreneur or simply a person who wants to be taken seriously and make a difference, this program speaks to the *real* salesperson in you.

Format: Public seminar or in-house training

Duration: Two days

Register your interest now!
Email: outlaw@boomsales.com.au

Learn more with practical advice from our experts

WILEY

The Art of Deliberate Success
David Keane

Power Stories
Valerie Khoo

Dealing with the Tough Stuff
Darren Hill, Alison Hill and Dr Sean Richardson

The One Thing
Creel Price

Play a Bigger Game
Rowdy McLean

First Be Nimble
Graham Winter

Building High Performance Business Relationships
Tony Lendrum

The Power of Influence
Sarah Prout

Communication in the Workplace
Baden Eunson

Available in print and e-book formats